God's Kingdom First

Professor Samuel C. Obi

authorHOUSE®

AuthorHouse™
1663 Liberty Drive
Bloomington, IN 47403
www.authorhouse.com
Phone: 1 (800) 839-8640

Published by AuthorHouse   11/10/2015

ISBN: 978-1-5049-5920-9 (sc)
ISBN: 978-1-5049-5921-6 (e)

Print information available on the last page.

Any people depicted in stock imagery provided by Thinkstock are models,
and such images are being used for illustrative purposes only.
Certain stock imagery © Thinkstock.

This book is printed on acid-free paper.

Because of the dynamic nature of the Internet, any web addresses or
links contained in this book may have changed since publication and
may no longer be valid. The views expressed in this work are solely those
of the author and do not necessarily reflect the views of the publisher,
and the publisher hereby disclaims any responsibility for them.

Scripture quotations marked KJV are from the Holy Bible, King James
Version (Authorized Version). First published in 1611. Quoted from the KJV
Classic Reference Bible, Copyright © 1983 by The Zondervan Corporation.

TABLE OF CONTENTS

Chapter 3

Chapter 4

Chapter 9

Preface

This book is written for all the folks who really want to see true success in their Christian lives. One of the secrets to living a truly successful godly life is by knowing what God's children are expected to do, and doing it. In Matthew 6:10, Jesus prayed for God's Kingdom to come, and that His will would be done on earth as it is done in heaven. In verse 33, He advised us to **seek first the kingdom and righteousness of God**, and then all the other things we need in life would be given to us as well. Many God's children do not think about this important topic, and then wonder why their lives are often in a state of doldrums, uninteresting and disorder. This book discusses what the Kingdom of God is, why it is important, and how we can seek it.

In Proverbs 9:10, the wisest man that ever lived declared that the fear of the LORD is the beginning of wisdom, and that the knowledge of the Holy One is understanding. In Proverbs 7:4-8, he told us to get wisdom and understanding no matter their cost. If we cherish and honor wisdom, she will exalt and embrace us. Seeking God's Kingdom is clearly the wisest thing any human being can do if we understand the real implications behind those words.

This book will be good for anyone who wants or needs to change his or her life for good, and for Christians who want to experience continued successful living in their Christian lives. The results of switching from a world of darkness into a world of light cannot even be described. The Kingdom of God will usher in a life of purpose, success and meaningfulness unmatched by no other.

The contents of this book are not new but have revealing secrets to a Christian's successful life in the Kingdom of God. Chapter 1 introduces the reader to the Kingdom of God, including what it looks like, how it is different from other world's kingdoms, and its many characteristics. Chapter 2 discusses the value or preciousness of the Kingdom of God, pointing out the fact that it has no comparison with anything else in the world. Chapter 3 delves into the powerfulness and transformative nature of the Word of God. It points out that only the Word of God has the power to penetrate, clean and transform any life, no matter how sinful.

Chapter 4 examines the deep and boundless love, mercy and grace of God and His expectation that we treat others the same. It reveals that God loves mankind with such an indescribable love, and that He also expects mankind to show a similar love to other human beings. The responsibility, preparedness and accountability that God wants His children to have regarding His Kingdom are discussed in chapter 5. This chapter points out that God wants us to be ready not just for the rapture but for a host of other things that involve responsibility and accountability. It also emphasizes that to whom much is given much is expected. Chapter 6 brings home the fact that God's children are living amongst the weed or non-Christian people of the world. As such, Christians must learn to live in certain manners. Chapter 7 discusses other important characteristics of the Kingdom of God, including miracles, progress, peace, joy, salvation, God's will, faith, and light. The all-important topic of opportunities in the Kingdom of God is discussed in chapter 8, and noted that opportunities are for the benefits of God's children and should be sought, but should be used for the glory of God. Chapter 9 is included for those who are not yet Christians who want to accept Christ as their Lord and Savior. It is only by accepting Him as one's Lord and Savior that the blessings and riches discussed in this book can become truly active in a person's life.

It is also noted here that a capital "K" has been used in this book when referring to the Kingdom of God. A lower case "k" is used when referring to other world's kingdoms. That way, it is easier to differentiate between God's Kingdom and man's or world's kingdoms. However, God's Kingdom also includes all the other smaller kingdoms. So it makes it clear who is actually in charge in this – man, demons, Satan, or God.

Professor Samuel C. Obi
San Jose State University
San Jose, California.

November, 2015.

Acknowledgements

I give all the credit to God who inspired the topic of this book, provided me with the opportunities to live, know Him, and gain the knowledge and information to write this book. All glory and honor belong to Him for ever and ever. May His name be hallowed. To those who helped in my Christian upbringing (parents, relations, mentors, teachers, pastors, friends etc.), words can never be enough to express my gratitude for the roles you played in my life.

My spiritual, moral, professional, and academic teachers, mentors, supporters, and advisors deserve mention here as well. It must be noted that I might not have remained a Christian today without their assistance in grooming and pruning me through life. Also my native town relations, mentors, sponsors, supporters, and the cultural and religious milieu there provided the foundational base of my beginning and sustained endurance in the spiritual pursuits that have lasted all my life. Some have gone on now to glory, but history will not fail to remember them for the sacrificial seed they sowed in me from my birth.

My late parents Chief Gabriel Ilechukwu Obi (Akunne) and Mrs. Virginia U. Obi helped to ensure that I embraced Christianity from the moment I was born. My late aunt and godmother Mrs. Winifred O. Obi helped to build and strengthen my spiritual life by ensuring that I read and memorized the scriptures, attended church and Christian activities, and participated in the daily morning and evening devotions that took place in her house during the six years I lived with her as a young boy. Her son and his wife Pastors Azuka and Ifeyinwa Obi later helped to reinforce that spiritual base when they allowed me to witness their zeal and sacrifice for Christ during the two years I lived with them as a young Christian.

My American Pastors, Christian mentors and family friends also helped in no small measures to my seeing Christ in deeper ways. Some sacrificed for me in so many ways, including their friendship, financial assistance, advising, mentoring and counseling when I was in college. Space cannot permit me here to mention the names of these numerous others who touched my life in so many ways that helped me to find a stronger anchor in Christ. The front cover image was generously provided by AuthorHouse through Thinkstock.com. I am grateful to this company for furnishing this nice image upon request.

Finally, but not the least, I want to thank my wife Dr. Adora Obi whose encouraging words, prayers, insights, and assistance during the writing and its review process helped in putting this book together. This book would not have been possible without her help.

Professor Samuel C. Obi
San Jose State University
San Jose, California.

November, 2015.

CHAPTER 1

Introduction to the Kingdom of God

The Creator's Goal

The Bible described the meticulous manner with which God created the earth and everything in it. He created the heaven and the earth, the seas and oceans, the animals including land, sea and flying animals of all kinds, the stars and all the heavenly bodies. Finally in the sixth day, He made man. He created them male and female; He also blessed them and named them "Mankind" (Genesis 1:27). In Genesis 2:15-24, He put them in the Garden of Eden to be managers of it according to specific rules and commands. Later, God commanded the people He created to multiply and fill the earth.

It is clear that God's intent in His creation was to have a Kingdom in which He was the only King. His prime motive was to have a loving relationship with mankind, His wonderful creation. And what better place to enjoy this relationship than in His Kingdom. Thus, He placed Adam and Eve in the most beautiful part of His Kingdom - the Garden of Eden. Their role there was basically to enjoy life in all its fullness. It is said in Genesis 3:8 that the Lord God walked in the garden in the cool of the day.

By definition, a kingdom constitutes a geographically located and inhabitable facility, palace, place, village, town, city, state or country with clearly defined boundary in which a ruler, chief, prince, princess, duke, duchess, king, queen, governor, prime minister, or president is in control. Clearly, the creation of the heaven and earth and everything in them is the first of any kingdom ever recorded in human history. Every other kingdom that has ever existed emerged out of this first Kingdom. The stories and histories about old and past empires, dominions, and kingdoms all came and died after this first Kingdom. The present slew of world's countries, unions, states and kingdoms all grew out of history after that first Kingdom. Thus, whether all these kingdoms know it or not, God is still the Ruler of all the kingdoms of the earth (2 Chronicles 20:6).

The growth in world's population and the resultant increase in the number of world's communities like villages, towns, and countries are all in accordance with God's command to His creation to multiply and fill the earth. While there are literally hundreds, if not thousands, of kingdoms in the world today, it is clear that God had great plans for the first Kingdom He created. For one thing, it was the largest geographical kingdom that has ever existed as one kingdom, even though it had very few humans living in it at the beginning. It showed that God's thoughts and plans for man are always big ones. While that same Kingdom has now been changed into many smaller geographically different tribal and ethnic communities, His plans for His Kingdom never changed. While mankind may have changed a few things in God's original plan, God's grand plans for mankind still remain the same.

However, mankind has veered terribly off the course in the process of inhabiting the earth. This happened at various times in world's history. The first recorded event of folks veering off the course of God's plan was when Adam and Eve ate the fruit that God clearly warned them not to eat. This is called disobedience. This resulted in God kicking them out of the garden and imposing some stiff penalties. The consequences of this sin did not end there but continued to this day. Their son Cain soon afterward murdered his brother Abel. Since then, mankind has been involved in the commission of multitudes of different kinds of sin. The pollution introduced by Adam and Eve affected their offspring throughout the generations to this day.

Another occasion of God's creation veering off the course of His intent was when Lucifer revolted against God in heaven. Again, this revolt resulted in him being kicked out of heaven and thrown into the earth (Luke 10:18; Isaiah 14:12; Ezekiel 28:16-17). Since then, Lucifer (also known as Satan) and his cohorts of revolted angels and demons have taken advantage of man's weakness to confuse, lie and cause many people to live bad and destructive lifestyles. Through their influence, we have seen laws changed to suit certain groups, new philosophies introduced to suit certain lifestyles, and all sorts of new opinions generated and supported to allow folks to do what they want irrespective of whether they are good or not.

But for whatever reasons all the numerous other world's kingdoms are established, founded or organized, mankind must know that God's Kingdom should not be compared to man's kingdoms. God's Kingdom is special in many ways, including the following examples:

1. God's Kingdom is greater and comprises this world and every other known world, planet or heavenly body.
2. God is the King of His Kingdom.
3. God cannot share His glory with anyone else, be they kings, leaders etc.
4. God demands holiness and righteousness in His Kingdom.
5. God has control over what happens in every other kingdom.
6. God often allows mankind to make choices regarding their earthly kingdoms.

The Role of Abraham

Yes, historically, our world has been ladened with sin and its results on mankind. Even so, God never gives up on His creation and His Kingdom. Even in those dark and miserable times, He always has good children He could count on. That was the nature of a man by the name of Abraham who was literally called a friend of God. God uses such individuals to teach His wayward children that it is possible to keep His commandments in spite of the turmoil that sin has brought into the world.

Thus God called Abraham out of his sinful folks and asked him to leave his people behind and to go to the land of Canaan which God would later give him and his descendants. God's plan was to rehabilitate His polluted Kingdom using this man Abraham. Abraham enjoyed a wonderful relationship with God. He told Abraham that He would make him the father of many nations (kingdoms) and that his descendants would be like the stars in number. That promise was fulfilled in the number and the nations of the people of the Jewish and Arabic folks during the past and present years. From Israelites, Ishmaelites, Edomites, Arabic states, and others, Abraham received that promise from the Lord.

The Bible is replete with the story of how Abraham's descendants struggled to finally occupy the Promised Land, also referred to as the land of Canaan. For many generations, Abraham's descendants multiplied, migrated, and eventually occupied the Promised Land. Through the descendants of Isaac, Jacob, Esau, and their children, their number increased. During the period of some 400 years while Jacob's children lived in Egypt, the Jews multiplied so much that they constituted a formidable force, so powerful that they defeated many powerful nations on their way to, and inside, the Promised Land. Through the leadership of Moses and Joshua, they conquered and occupied the land of promise.

When David later became the king of Israel, he expanded and consolidated the kingdom and made it the most powerful nation of its time. King David also enjoyed a great relationship with God. Much of the book of Psalms was written by him alone. In Psalm 42:1-2, he longingly noted that as a deer panted after the water brook, so his soul longed for the living God. During his reign, Israel became the most God-fearing nation of its time. In everything done during King David's reign, God was the center. No king in Israel's history made Israel to be closer to God as King David did. Israel became the centerpiece of the kind of kingdom God had originally intended for His people. As a result of this, Israel was flourishing economically, politically, and militarily. She defeated all her enemies. When David's son Solomon became the next king after his father, he became the wisest and richest man that has ever lived in all the earth. Kings visited him from different nations just to hear his wisdom. Never in world's history has there been anything like that.

But sin still has its recourse. Some of the kings that succeeded David were not as godly. Prophet after prophet warned the nation about the consequences, but they did not change their course. As a result, the country went to various periods of defeat and captivity. The Assyrians, Babylonians, Egyptians, Philistines, Romans and others defeated them at various times in history, took them to exile where they lived for many years as second-class citizens. The Bible contains a record of these captivities. Sometimes, some of the captives received a reprieve from their captors and returned home to Israel. Still, God never gives up on His people and His plan. Mankind may waddle, suffer, live and die in their sin, but God never gives up hope on His plan and His people.

By the time of Christ, who was Himself a direct descendant of Abraham and David, Israel had already been under the Roman rule for many years. His folks were still expecting a Messiah that was promised to them by Moses. They were expecting a conquering Messiah who would be strong and powerful like King David. But God had a different kind of Messiah in mind.

Jesus' Kind of Kingdom

King David did prophesy about Jesus Christ when he said that the Lord said to his Lord: "Sit at my right hand until I make your enemies a footstool for your feet". He also said that the Lord would extend Christ's mighty scepter from Zion, saying, "Rule in the midst of your enemies!" (Psalm 110:1-2). Kind David was actually prophetically referring to the coming of Christ. When Jesus finally came into the scene, He made it clear to everyone that His Kingdom was not of this world. He was a suffering Messiah and not a conquering Messiah. Throughout His ministry on earth, He emphasized grace, love, mercy, truth, service, His Father and the Kingdom of God. He ended up establishing Christianity which is today the greatest, richest, most humane, most powerful, most useful, and the most predominant religion in the world.

Jesus clearly suggested there was a coming Kingdom as well as a present or as-is kingdom. The as-is kingdom is the current state of Christianity in an imperfect world. It is

Christianity in a world filled with sin, wars, hunger, killings, hate, unfairness, anarchy, slavery, intolerance, hardships, abuse of power, joblessness, poverty, and numerous others. The to-be Kingdom is just the opposite of the as-is kingdom. Not only that this Kingdom will have no religious diversity as we currently have, but there will be no deaths, sicknesses, sufferings, torture, hunger, diseases, fear, killings, wars and other evils. This kingdom will be full of joy and unspeakable glory, the half of which has never yet been told.

Christ made it clear through the apostle Paul that the Kingdom of God was not meat and drink, but righteousness in the Holy Spirit (Romans 14:17). By saying this, Paul was basically reminding people the original intent of God. God is a righteous God and does not deal in any kind of unrighteousness. God's original promise and plan still stand, but it must be undertaken in His terms. His demand for truth and righteousness still stands. No amount of human depravity and downfall can change God's plans and promises. He is also fulfilling His words that:

1. Man shall not live by bread alone, but by every word that comes out of the mouth of God (Matthew 4:4).
2. God should be worshiped in spirit and in truth (John 4:24).

Meat and drink? How pointed and true Paul's statement is. World's kingdoms always stress meat and drink. This goes beyond ordinary delicious, tasty and expensive foods and wines which money can buy. It actually includes a whole lot more. Meat and drink here include riches and all the things people die to get in this world. God's Kingdom is not about "all these other things". **God's Will is FIRST about His Kingdom and His righteousness**. His Kingdom and His righteousness go hand in hand. The two cannot be separated because they coexist together. You cannot have one without the other.

That is why His presence is always experienced whenever there is any of those two present anywhere. Abraham loved God in an idolatrous town of Ur of the Chaldeans and God visited him there to give him a message that would turn the world upside down for good. David was just a lad tending his father's "few" sheep, but God sent a prophet by the name of Samuel to find him there and anoint him to be the king of Israel, an experience that gave Israel its best years ever since throughout its history.

Jesus said in Luke 9:27 that some of the folks standing with Him while He ministered at a place near a city called Bethsaida would not die before they saw the Kingdom of God. By this He meant that receiving Him as one's savior is the same as seeing the Kingdom of God. Why is this?

What Happens in a Kingdom?

It should be clear from the foregoing discussions that God clearly expects certain things to be happening in His Kingdom. The book of Genesis chapter 1 has the story of how God created the heavens and the earth. In verse 27, He created mankind. In verse 28, He blessed them (Adam and Eve) and said to them to be fruitful and increase in number; fill the earth and subdue it. He also told them to rule over the fish in the sea and the birds in the sky and over every living creature that moves on the ground. In verse 31, He saw that everything He had made was good.

Just like all world's leaders, God expects us to live in peace, obey Him, love and respect our fellow human beings, and enjoy life in its fullness. For a full information about what was in God's mind about what mankind should be doing in His Kingdom, just take a look at the 10 commandments as specified in Exodus 20:2-17 and Deuteronomy 5:6-21:

1. You shall have no other gods before Me.
2. You shall not make idols.
3. You shall not take the name of the LORD your God in vain.
4. Remember the Sabbath day, to keep it holy.
5. Honor your father and your mother.
6. You shall not murder.
7. You shall not commit adultery.
8. You shall not steal.
9. You shall not bear false witness against your neighbor.
10. You shall not covet.

Several key things are clear from God's intents and commandments:

1. God wants humans to live in this world and to enjoy it.
2. God wants humans to reproduce and multiply.
3. God wants humans to take care of this world.
4. In fulfilling the first three, God wants humans to be responsible and play by the rules, hence the Ten

Commandments and all His other laws, precepts and principles.

In fulfilling the above wishes of God, mankind has to encounter a whole lot of issues involving different dealings with fellow humans on a day-to-day basis. Often these issues cause mankind to clash with fellow mankind. God knows that it would be impossible for mankind to successfully accomplish all their wishes, challenges and wants in this world without first following His laws. For example, if there was no commandment to love fellow humans as themselves, there would have been more killings in this world than have already been witnessed. The world would be such a barbaric place that survival would be nearly impossible. The evils of the holocaust, ethnic cleansings and other world's genocides would pale in comparison to the atrocities that would have been committed in this world today, i.e. assuming that there would still be a human being left in this world.

Consequently, God expects His creation to live a life that pleases Him. His Kingdom is not meat and drinks but righteousness and holy living which include goodness, good behavior, right living, ethical living and godly living. He longs for His creation to live the most holy lives that please Him. He must be pleased first before we please man. He longs that we live not to please others or to justify ourselves, but to live in truth in our innermost being.

Our Lord's Prayer on this Topic

Jesus clearly showed the oneness and the supremacy of God and His kingdom when He taught His disciples how to pray

(Matthew 6:9-13). The first three lines cut deftly into this issue as follows:

Our Father in heaven,
hallowed be Your name,
Your Kingdom come.

In this prayer, Christ recognized the prime position of our Father God (first line). No other god or leader has ever been recognized or elevated like that. When they are, they are usually localized and they are usually described in the form of animals, trees, mountains, planets, superstitions or evil spirits. The first line also indicated the singularity of the only true God.

In the second line, Jesus suggested how God's name should be treated. To hallow means to honor someone as holy or sacred; to make holy, to worship, or to greatly revere or respect. This level of respect is reserved for God only. If mankind receives this kind of honor, then there is no other reverence that will differentiate that person from God.

Because only God's Kingdom can provide the type of perfection mankind is seeking, Jesus prayed in line three that God's Kingdom come. He nailed His points home with the last few lines of the full version of the Lord's Prayer by stating that: "For Thine is the Kingdom, and the power, and the glory, for ever and ever!" Yes the Kingdom, power and glory belong only to God. God's Kingdom is the ultimate perfection which no other leader, ruler, king or president can provide. This is the only place where there is perfect peace, joy, love and everything man can ever wish to have.

The happiest, richest and most powerful people in this world do not even come close to the joys, riches and power of the folks who will be in the Kingdom of God.

The Nature and Characteristics of the Kingdom of God

As has been discussed in previous sections, the basic nature of God's Kingdom is goodness in all its forms. It is the only good kingdom there is if there is any at all. Kingdoms have come and gone throughout history. Today, there are modern types of kingdoms in the forms of nations, states, and royals or royalties. Some of the things they all have in common are corruption, inefficiency, mortality and all the other limitations of mankind. But a quick examination of the nature of God's Kingdom shows quite the opposite.

The Coming Kingdom and the Present Kingdom

The future kingdom is a perfect place, full of peace, love and life everlasting. The apostle John described it in Revelation 21:2 when he saw the Holy City, the New Jerusalem, coming down out of heaven from God, prepared as a bride beautifully dressed for her husband. He noted in Revelation 22:5 that there will be no night there, and that the folks living there will not need the light of a lamp or the light of the sun because God will give them light.

But the Bible made it clear that there is also a Kingdom of God in this world. This Kingdom has been expanding since its establishment in spite of all the satanic oppositions and roadblocks against it. There have been other religions founded by the enemy for the sole purpose of fighting against God's Kingdom. This present and growing kingdom is often referred, compared, or related to in the descriptions Jesus gave about the nature of God's Kingdom. In other words, our present world is striving to be like God's Kingdom.

It is now a two-thousand-plus year old war. It is no secret that Jesus ushered in that Kingdom when He introduced Christianity to the world. The war that Jesus went through in establishing His Kingdom was indescribable to say the least. He was fiercely, jealously, wickedly and lawlessly attacked by the rulers of His day who wanted to do away with Him. The High Priest concocted one of the most horrible lies ever invented by mankind in his bid to get Him crucified. Pilate the governor neglected one of the most basic human rights in his attempt to preserve his job and friendship with the status quo. Even Jesus' disciples committed some of the unexpected disappointments during His passion by betraying, deserting, denying and abandoning the One they had loved for three years. The events surrounding His apprehension, trial and crucifixion were some of the most immoral, cruel and unethical abuses of power in human history.

The above treatments to the most righteous person that ever lived on planet earth can only be pointing at one fact: that world's kingdoms have come short of perfection and only needs a Redeemer who would save it from the only penalty left to it. That penalty would have been death. But Jesus preferred to die for mankind because of His love for us. So, in giving His life for mankind, He also established a Kingdom of grace, love and peace for the same folks that crucified Him. He even called on His Father God to forgive them for they knew not what they were doing.

Since the establishment of the Church, Christianity has been growing and improving. It is not perfect but it has been getting better. While there is still a lot to be done, Christianity has reached every corner of the world, has in various ways helped the poor and hungry more than any organization has in history, has literally brought life to many world communities in the forms of religion, education and hospitals. Its influence has helped to evangelize numerous communities, and ushered in numerous amenities and removed millions of idols and idol practices in this world. No religion can boast of that.

The Nature of God's Kingdom

One way to look at the Kingdom of God is by considering what Jesus said in Matthew 12:28-29. He noted to the Pharisees who spitefully suggested He was casting out demons through the power of Beelzebub, that it was not so because if it was by the Spirit of God that He drove out demons, then the Kingdom of God had come upon them. He asked them to explain how in the world anyone could enter a strong man's house and carry off his possessions if he was not stronger than the strong man to begin with.

This suggests that the Kingdom of God is associated with healings, miracles and good spectacular occurrences that cannot be found anywhere else. The Kingdom of God overcomes evil in all its forms, resulting in miracles as demons cannot inhabit in the Kingdom of God. It takes a stronger man to enter, overcome and plunder the house of another man.

Some of the godly folks who influenced others in their lives certainly helped to usher in the Kingdom of God. Consider persons like the patriarchs, saints, apostles, or modern missionaries, for example. Abraham, the apostle Paul, David Livingstone, Mother Theresa, and Billy Graham all lived with and ministered to millions of folks in their days. It was said of them that they literally lived out their lives for the people they labored for. Their lives resulted in the conversions of millions of people into Christianity and in the construction of many churches, schools and hospitals to name just a few.

In a similar way, millions of Christians interact with and influence other people for good. Christians actively do this everyday in their workplaces, churches, schools, governments, neighborhoods, streets, market places and all the other places where all the sundry activities are undertaken. In each case, good positive results take place.

God's Kingdom is greater than any kingdom on the earth. And it will always prevail against any power on earth. It has positive transformation power which has been manifested in different ways throughout history. Hence, it is the single most important thing that is worth seeking in the world today.

Christ also declared in John 12:24 that His Kingdom would reign forever. Some Greek visitors had come to see Jesus through His disciples. When Jesus was told about this, He declared that He was about to be glorified and that He was about to establish His Kingdom. He was basically referring to the founding of Christianity. Christianity has taken root and has been expanding ever since. He also noted that His Father would honor those who serve Him (verse 26). This means that all those who diligently live for Christ will never be disappointed. Christ also pointed out that when He is lifted up on the cross, he would draw all men unto Himself (John 12:32-33). He said this to show the kind of death He was about to die.

The following sections describe the characteristics and nature of the Kingdom of God which distinguish it from any entity, event or phenomenon in the world today. His Kingdom is characteristically different and unique in every way imaginable. They will lead all who discover them into deeper relationship with God. And in so doing, these folks will reap the rich benefits promised to everyone who obeys.

Characteristics of God's Kingdom

Another way to understand the kingdom of God is by examining the parables told by Christ during His ministry on earth. His parables have deep meanings and shed some light into the Kingdom of God from different perspectives. Twelve of these parables are taken from the book of Matthew and are chronologically listed here for this book:

- The parable of the weeds (Matthew 12:24-52).
- The parable of the sower (Matthew 13:3-9).
- The parable of the mustard seed (Matthew 13:31).
- The parable of the hidden treasure (Matthew 12:44).

- The parable of the leaven (Matthew 13:33).
- The parable of the merchant seeking beautiful pearls (Matthew 13:45-46).
- The parable of the dragnet (Matthew 13:47).
- The parable of the king and the unforgiving servant (Matthew 18:21-35).
- The parable of the landowner who went out early in the morning to hire laborers for his vineyard (Matthew 20:1-16).
- The parable of the king who prepared a great wedding for his son (Matthew 22:1-14).
- The parable of the ten virgins (Matthew 25:1-13).
- The parable of the man who gave talents to his servants (Matthew 25:14-30).

These parables can be roughly categorized into five groups as follows:

1. The value or preciousness of the kingdom of God. (This is illustrated by the parable of the hidden treasure and the parable of pearl of great price).
2. The powerfulness and transformative nature of the Word of God. (This is illustrated by the parable of the mustard seed, the parable of the leaven, and the parable of the sower).
3. The deep and boundless love, mercy and grace of God and His expectation that we treat others the same way. (This is illustrated by the parable of the king and the unforgiving servant, and the parable of the landowner who went out early in the morning to hire laborers for his vineyard).

4. The responsibility, accountability and preparedness that God wants His children to have regarding His Kingdom. (This is illustrated by the parable of the sower, the parable of the king who prepared a great wedding for his son, the parable of the ten virgins, and the parable of the man who gave talents to his servants).

5. God's children living amongst the weed or non-Christian people of the world. (This is illustrated by the parable of the weed and the parable of the dragnet).

From these groupings emerge what have been labeled as the characteristics of God's Kingdom in this chapter. The categories show what God's Kingdom is like, what He expects of His children, and the nature of the world in which we live. They are so important that each will be discussed in more details in the following chapters of this book.

In summary, this chapter described the Creator's goal of having a loving relationship with mankind, His wonderful creation. And what better place to enjoy this relationship than in His Kingdom. The chapter looked into the means God used to accomplish this goal, including the roles of Abraham and the Lord Jesus Christ. There was also a discussion about what happens in a kingdom and about Jesus' kind of kingdom. Our Lord's Prayer and teachings on this topic were also explored. The chapter emphasized the importance of seeking first the Kingdom of God and His righteousness.

It has also been shown that God's Kingdom has no match and is the ultimate Kingdom. It was planned from time immemorial, and God is the only King and Lord in it. It has nothing but big and beautiful characteristics, such as the value or preciousness of the Kingdom of God, the powerfulness and transformative nature of the Word of God, the deep and boundless love, mercy and grace of God, His expectation that we treat other the same way He treats us, the preparedness that God wants His children to have regarding His Kingdom, the accountability and responsibility God expects of His children, and the awareness that God's children are living amongst the weed or non-Christian people of the world.

The next chapter will continue the discussions by examining in more detail the specific characteristic of the value or preciousness of the Kingdom of God. The discussions there will help to shed more light into what God really thinks about His Kingdom in relation to man. This understanding will also help Christians to know more about how they ought to live their lives in this day and age.

Chapter 2

The Value or Preciousness of the Kingdom of God

For the most part, this book is actually about the topic discussed in this chapter i.e. the value of the Kingdom of God. It has been discussed variously that the Kingdom of God MUST be sought first by anyone who wants to get anything from God. The two parables (the hidden treasure and the pearl of great price) simply highlight this point. In this world, people do just about anything to get things like money, education, career or other things of value. There are folks who sold their only piece of property in order to get some education or a business opportunity. These are things that constitute value to these folks.

But the fact is that these worldly things that we think are of so much value to us are really nothing compared to the preciousness of the Kingdom of God. This point was exactly what Jesus was trying to illustrate in the two parables: The parable of the hidden treasure and the parable of pearl of

21

great price. No amount of money or anything of value that we spent or lost in order to find the Kingdom of God is ever too much. Finding God's Kingdom is beyond value, and every wise person should try and find it first.

Yes, we all have things we attach different degrees of value to in life. But the argument here is that none of those earthly values should be compared to the value of God's Kingdom. It should take a higher place in our daily pursuit. That is what Christ was trying to point out throughout His ministry on earth. Consider the case of an earthly king whose kingdom is in a state of disarray. Imagine what would be the attitude of this king toward those of his subjects who are trying to bring disorder to his kingdom. If earthly kings understand the importance of growing their kingdoms, how much more do you think God would like to grow His? By far, on a higher level, the health, peace, prosperity and growth of God's Kingdom is far more important to Him than anything else we do. And anyone who can "help" Him to build His Kingdom is indeed God's good friend.

All that Glitter is not Gold

Humans, including adults, are very much like babies in our wants and needs for the things of this world. We treasure many things including jewelry, money, nice cars, good homes, good jobs, education, status and such likes. Some even venture to have multiple units of these, and sometimes become millionaires or billionaires. In the rush to acquire all these, we have a tendency to forget that while these things help to make life on earth more enjoyable, they are not the end of it all. They are just temporary things that tend to satisfy for a while. Like the babies mentioned above, they glitter and attract our eyes for a while. And for a while, we are happy as we successfully pursue and acquire these things for the moment.

One of the saddest passages in the Bible is the story or parable of the rich fool described in Luke 12:16-21. In his bid to enlarge his worldly riches, this man planned to tear down his barns and build bigger ones where he would store his surplus grain. His ultimate goal was nothing else but to take life easy and eat, drink and be merry. He completely forgot about God who made it possible for him to get the increase in the first place. The passage indicated that God called him a fool, and informed him that his life would be taken from him that night.

While the Lord Jesus had some rich friends, He was particularly heavy handed on the rich of this world. In His encounter with the young rich ruler described in Matthew 19:16-22, He bluntly said that it was easier for a camel to go through the eye of a needle than for a rich person to enter the kingdom of God. The reason for these warnings is because of the glittering forces of riches. Glittering makes one to forget his or her bearing. Two of the definitions of glittering are *impressively successful or elaborate* and *Brilliant or showy, often superficial attractiveness*. When someone is rich, it is very difficult to be humble or obey the rules of God. Rich people have a tendency to depend on their wealth more than on God. Christ said in Luke 12:34 that a person's heart will be where their treasure is.

The Lord admonished us to make God's Kingdom number one in our lives. Some people are able to find an answer to this issue early in life, but it would appear that most people do not. Some find this answer later on in their lives. And many do not find it at all till they die. One way to illustrate the value and preciousness of the Kingdom of God is to observe the lives of those who have genuinely found it. Two stories will be used to illustrate this phenomenon.

Zacchaeus the Chief Tax Collector and the Apostle Paul

A typical example that was mentioned in the New Testament was a man by the name of Zacchaeus (Luke 19:1-10). Luke described this man as a chief tax collector who was wealthy, a typical economic achievement of their time. But it was clear this man was not contented with himself in spite of all his wealth. Something was bothering him. He still wanted to see who Jesus was, something many rich people of our time do not have time for. The crowd following Jesus that day was heavy, but because he was short and could not see over the crowd, Zacchaeus climbed a sycamore-fig tree to see Jesus. When the Lord saw him up there, he proposed a meeting at Zacchaeus' house. Jesus must have seen in this man something that is rare to see in many rich folks. The Lord sees the hearts of people and He knows who is ready for His Kingdom and who is not.

In the encounter with Zacchaeus, Jesus did not even need to preach because the man immediately proposed to give half of his possessions to the poor and to pay back four times to anyone the amount he had cheated them. Upon seeing this magnitude of evidence, the Lord declared that salvation had come to Zacchaeus' house that day. It is clear in this story that wealth comes after the Kingdom since the Kingdom is far greater and more important than anything else.

Years later, the apostle Paul would have a similar life transformation, but from a different perspective. He was full of zeal for his Judaism religion and had been empowered by Jewish authority to arrest and imprison Christians after the death and resurrection of Jesus Christ. On his way to Damascus, he ran into Jesus in a rather traumatic experience (Acts 9:3-4). His life took a dramatic turn from there and he started calling Jesus "Lord" for the rest of his life. He abandoned his original mission and became one of the leaders of the early Church. It is the same Paul who later said in Philippians 3:8 that he considered everything a loss because of the surpassing worth of knowing Christ Jesus his Lord, for whose sake he has lost all things and considered them garbage that he may gain Christ.

Our Modern Day Elites

In our modern time, untold numbers of men and women are finding out that this world has a lot that glitter but are not gold. There was a man who is one of the few Nigerian Christian leaders whose lives do, in many ways, parallel that of the apostle Paul. His conversion and born-again experience took place at a time when Nigeria was budding into her first spiritual renaissance of the early to late 1970s, which characterized Nigeria immediately after Nigeria's Civil War. Young, handsome, highly educated in England as a lawyer with a terminal degree, and hailing from a royal family and with great anchors on both sides of his parents' families, he had it all. But something was not sitting quite well inside of him. This was a time when nothing short of no-nonsense Christianity attitude was the only way to really save a person, and he took it on. He clearly knew where the treasure was. His story reflects what happened to numerous other modern day elites of our time.

His departure from the worldly norms was shocking to his friends and relatives. "How could a person who had such great opportunities decide to abandon them and become tangled with the unpopular and unattractive Christianity of the day?" they wondered. But many would later follow along the same route, after discovering that this man was running the race of his life. Over the years, that number gradually increased and included folks from every clan and clime, including many from his immediate and extended family. More so, no one can ever tell the number of the numerous others who found the Lord through the direct and indirect ministration efforts of this servant of God.

Early on, after discovering "the secret of a happy yielded life", as he phrased it in one of his tracts, he started out very humbly, attending a Bible college in Nigeria to train to become a pastor. This was the initial proof to all that his was a serious commitment to God. Few top Nigerian British-educated lawyers in those days could be so humble to do that. But like the apostle Paul, he counted all that but dung for the excellency of knowing his Lord. Upon graduation from Bible school, he became a pastor and was literally on a trajectory-like upward mobility in the church's ranks ever since, as the church kept promoting him from one level to another. He made it to the zenith where he held some of the highest titles of his church

He preached Jesus on Lagos streets, other Nigerian cities, in the churches, workplaces, prayer meetings, in small and great crusades, camp meetings and around the world. His theme to everyone was that "This world means nothing without Jesus Christ". He published numerous tracts and books, and broadcasted God's message on televisions, radios and other media to spread the Word to as many people as he could reach. He also became the Belteshazzar of his royal clan. He knew where the *treasure* was and did his best to reveal it to every one of his immediate and extended family members. Without a doubt, his uncompromising ministry helped to influence the decision by his Royal Family to remove and destroy their historic idols, and caused many non-Christian relatives to start attending churches and to be more spiritually engaged.

Seeking God's Kingdom First

In Matthew 6:33, Jesus asked us to first seek God's Kingdom and His righteousness, and all these other things will be given to us as well. Christ, the wisest Being that has ever lived as human on planet earth, has advised humans to "seek first" the Kingdom of God. Without mincing any word, this is the most useful piece of advice any human being can get from any person in the world today.

The word "seek" literally means to search for, or try to find, someone or something. The manner of its usage by the Lord in the passage suggests something to be sought for with all diligence and care irrespective of the cost, time and whatever it takes to find. Many people have done some unimaginable things as they searched for important lost belongings in their lives or in the lives of others. At one time, a lake was drained by the authorities of one county in California to search the water bed for a missing person. You can imagine the amount of resources (men and women, time, machines and all) the county utilized in accomplishing this mission.

Every human, organization or government has sought certain things that were important to their lives. Some people have gone some great lengths for opportunities to get some education. I know people whose families sacrificed valuable pieces of property like homes, lands and businesses for it. People have spent time and resources and traveled far and wide seeking things that were valuable to them. Oil and mineral companies travel far and spend a lot of money in research, technology, equipment and manpower seeking promising locations to drill for oil, gas and precious stones. In academia, educators and researchers spend an awful amount of time and manpower trying to find new information, new ideas and knowledge for advancing society and for product and service innovation.

In the same way, the Lord expects us to demonstrate a reasonable amount of effort when we do the type of search He is talking about here. In Matthew 7:7, He commanded us to seek and that we will find. When He sees how important the thing is to us, He usually reacts to our need. Consider the case of a barren woman by the name of Hannah who sought the Lord in prayers for quite some time. She sorrowed, grieved, wept and prayed, but her request was granted in the end. Usually, everyone that really seeks finds. It may not be exactly the way we want it, but the answer is generally better.

Seeking His Righteousness First

One of the toughest duties, and yet the main duty, of Christians is the task of remaining steadfastly focused on the command to seek God's righteousness. It is easier to say it than doing it. And it is easier to do it if it is something that can just be done once or twice in a day or so and no more. But the problem (and thus the challenge) is that we are required to continually keep doing it nonstop every minute, every hour, 24/7 and all the days of our lives. That is where it becomes a huddle for many Christians.

Consider the case of a young Christian woman who works as a teller at a bank where she interacts with hundreds of individuals everyday, including customers, colleagues, supervisors, friends and family members. This young lady has multitudes of challenges such as being respectful to customers and her bosses, controlling her emotions when customers or colleagues misunderstood her or told her boss something she did not do, and knowing how to say no when friends or coworkers want her to do something she does not want to do or go to a place she should not go.

Or consider the case of a Christian young man who found himself in the midst of a bunch of colleagues and friends telling nasty jokes at a party where liquor and beer were flowing freely. He did not want to leave the group because he did not want to offend his friends. And he did not want to be involved in their dirty jokes because he did not want to offend his God. He tried to change the conversation but instead another already loaded young man asked him why he is not drinking like others. He told them he doesn't drink and everyone roared into laughter until he almost felt ashamed.

The above scenarios are practical issues of life many Christians undergo on a daily basis. They are aspects and parts of Christianity's challenges in living the righteousness of God. While the livers (those living it) often know it is good for them and the kingdom, non-Christians and weak Christians often do not understand that. That is why Proverbs 1:10-15 warned God's children to not give in if sinful men entice them. It declares in verses 26-27 that wisdom will laugh and mock them when disaster strikes, when calamity overtakes them like a storm, when disaster sweeps them like a whirlwind, and distress and trouble overwhelm them. This narrative is typical of what happens to many people who live unrighteous lifestyles.

There is no exaggeration to the fact that righteous living really pays big dividends. I have lost numerous friends, relations, neighbors, and acquaintances in my life. Many of these losses were folks who lived lives of crime, uncontrolled drinking of liquor and alcohol, and other substance and lifestyle abuses like heavy use of drugs, tobacco or emotions. Some died as a result of reckless living like violence due to uncontrolled anger which led to fights, suicides, high blood pressure, aids, and organ failures. On the contrary, most good Christians that I know enjoy their lives, often to full age. They generally have goodness following them all their lives. While sometimes bad things happen to Christians, it is not often as a result of unrighteous living on their part.

Seeking God's righteousness is a continual and lifelong process. While it may be uncomfortable sometimes, the Lord wants us to maintain the lifestyle because it highlights His kingdom. The little discomfort we feel is worldly and is nothing compared to the benefits that result in the end. This discomfort is one of the reasons we are described as living sacrifices (Romans 12:1). Friends may laugh at Christians for taking a stand for righteous living, but in the end the same friends will seek out the Christians to help them out of their troubles.

All These Things will be Added to Us

The previous sections showed that God has a Kingdom and that His people should recognize it and make it the center of their lives. It is only when we do that first part that this section starts to take effect, i.e. "all these things will be added to us" as stated in Matthew 6:33. By all these things, Jesus meant all the cares and needs that we go about trying how to acquire, overcome or solve in this life: money, material things, education, spouses, children, friends, business opportunities, successful careers, good health, peace, jobs, protection, deliverance, victories, successes and every other good and perfect gift (James 1:17).

True and fulfilling riches of life come ONLY when we recognize and allow God to be the head and center of our lives. All godly Christians who make God's Kingdom first always bloom where they are planted. Two examples of

God's blessings to godly folks are provided here as it will be time- and space-consuming to try to mention the numerous other occasions.

Consider what the Psalmist said about wisdom in Psalm 119:98-100. He declared that God's commands are always with him (the Psalmist) and make him wiser than his enemies. He noted that he had more insight than all his teachers, because he meditated on God's statutes. He also stated that he had more understanding than the elders because he obeyed God's precepts. Clearly, the Psalmist is testifying what happened in his life as a result of his closeness to God's commands, statutes and precepts. Most people think that the biggest blessing is wisdom and knowledge, and this man got it all. Proverbs 4:7 noted that wisdom is of utmost importance, and that we should get it, and with all our effort we should work to acquire understanding. Psalm 111:10 declares that the fear of God is the beginning of wisdom, and that all who follow God's precepts have good understanding.

The Bible also noted a man by the name of Obed-Edom who was blessed because the Ark of the Covenant of God was kept in his house for just three months. The Bible also noted that a man by the name of Uzzah was struck dead by God because he touched the Ark inappropriately. When this happened, David became afraid of God and had to send the Ark to Obed-Edom's house (2 Samuel 6:1-12).

Many Christian leaders believe that Obed-Edom took good care of that Ark and attended and sacrificed to it as Moses had prescribed. As a result, the Lord blessed Obed-Edom's family so much that within a period of only three months David literally rushed back to get the Ark from Obed-Edom so that it would be located near his palace. "When those who were carrying the Ark of the Lord had taken six steps, he (David) sacrificed a bull and a fattened calf. Wearing a linen ephod, David was dancing before the Lord with all his might, while he and all Israel were bringing up the ark of the Lord with shouts and the sound of trumpets" (2 Samuel 6:13-15).

Obed-Edom must have done some special service to be blessed this way. I believe with all my heart that he was a very godly and honest man and that he followed Moses' laws to the letter in ministering to God's Ark in his house. He must have established some type of group praise worship, prayer and fellowship in his house. He must have taught the people about how to worship God and how to live righteously for Him. He must have been a godly man with a high level of godly virtues such as honesty, self-control, integrity, hard work, fairness, responsibility, trustworthiness, care, and faithfulness.

We Should be all About His kingdom

Everything we are involved in should be about God's Kingdom because God created them all. Whether we are in engineering, medicine, education, politics, law, science, sports, arts, military, leadership and various other careers, or whether we are students, unemployed, married, single, old or young, we should be all about God's Kingdom. Christians need to be participating in every type of job, career or business imaginable in this world. Most godly folks in the world are actually working in the secular world in just about every area of work. While they often don't tell their co-workers about God and His kingdom, their lives are being observed by their co-workers, many of whom are not Christians. The lives of Christians also shape the lives of their fellow workers just as their lives are influenced by those of their fellow workers. It is at this level of interaction that it is said that the tire hits the road. Then it becomes a life of a melting pot for good or for bad.

The above scenario often turns good for good Christians who truly seek God's Kingdom and His righteousness first. The truth of their lives will often influence their counterparts with such positive impacts that more hearts are changed for the Lord. Abraham had this type of experience when he was cohabiting with the Philistines at a place called Beersheba, when these folks saw how his life was different, and how God was blessing him. At that time, a king by the name of Abimelek and the commander of his forces named Phicol, concerned that the blessings of Abraham might have no boundary because of his godliness, said to Abraham, "God is with you in everything you do. Now swear to me here before God that you will not deal falsely with me or my children or my descendants. Show to me and the country where you now reside as a foreigner the same kindness I have shown to you" (Genesis 21: 22-24).

It was made clear in Genesis 21:34 and Genesis 26:12 that Abraham (and later on his son Isaac) was blessed in the land of the Philistines while he lived there. He and his son Isaac successfully dug so many wells and found water that the Philistines often stole their wells. In other words, they were able to find water when the Philistines could not find any. For folks whose lives depended on rearing livestock in those days, having good wells with water in them for human drinking and for watering their flocks was a must-have if they were to survive at a place. And the technology and skill of digging the wells themselves were not like what we have these days. Digging an average well in those days must have taken days of torturous efforts with expensive and crude tools by today's standards.

This chapter has endeavored to point out the fact that nothing else compares in value with the Kingdom of God. It is the number one thing mankind must seek, and then every other thing will be added to us. It points out the fact that all that glitters is not gold, and used different examples of personalities to illustrate men's efforts to seek the Kingdom of God. The next chapter will look into the powerfulness and transformative nature of the Word of God.

CHAPTER 3

The Powerfulness and Transformative Nature of the Word of God

The powerfulness and transformative nature of the Word of God illustrated by the parable of the mustard seed, the parable of the leaven, and the parable of the sower described in Matthew 13:3-9, Matthew 13:31 and Matthew 13:33 are the thrust of this chapter. Paul noted in Hebrews 4:12 that the Word of God is alive and active, and that it is sharper than any double-edged sword. He stated that the "Word of God penetrates even to dividing soul and spirit, joints and marrow; it judges the thoughts and attitudes of the heart". Proverbs 3:1 notes that the Word of God gives life. And in John 15:3, Jesus declared to His disciples that they were already clean because of the Word He spoke to them.

Only the Word of God has the power to reach human souls and perform the transformative miracles that change people who used to be bad into some of the best loving and caring people in the world. God's Word is truth and, as a result, it has the power to reach every human heart and cause positive changes to take place in every part of the world. Jesus prayed in John 17:17 for God to sanctify His disciples by the truth which is God's Word.

It should also be mentioned that the powerfulness of the Word of God does not just stop at changing people, it also causes those changed to expand or grow into more usefulness for the glory of God. Just as the mustard seed grew into one of the largest trees and the birds came and perched in its branches; and just as the leaven caused the dough to expand into hunger-quenching bread, the Word of God causes people to develop into better and greater folks than they used to be. By eating the Word of God on a daily basis, God's people can be transformed into greater instruments suitable for His service. However, people's hearts have to be prepared and ready to accept God's Word. The parable of the sower showed that some were not prepared and did not obtain the benefits.

This topic has some implications and challenges for God's children. The first is the transformation that should be taking place in our own lives. The second is what we can do with our changed lives. The next sections will discuss these implications in more details.

Christian Transformation

The transforming power of the Word of God changes even the hardest hearts. Its power makes grown men and women to cry. As it penetrates, it reaches every depth and breadth of life itself, causing complete cleansing of the most dirty lives. Prostitutes and murderers like the sinful woman who anointed Jesus' feet with perfume (Luke 7:36-50) and the apostle Paul who supervised the killing of Stephen (Acts 7:54-60) were transformed into the most beautifully clean and holy individuals. In our modern world, former armed robbers, alcoholics, drug addicts, thieves, liars, rapists, adulterers, unbelievers and all sorts of evil doers are constantly transformed by the Word of God.

Just about every successful minister of God and folks in both religious and secular organizations will testify that their lives weren't perfect when they started out in their careers. It took years of continual cleansing by God's Word to bring the improvements that made them the jewels of their professions. In the book of Philemon, the apostle Paul returned a man by the name of Onesimus to his master. Onesimus had stolen from his master but was transformed by the Word of God through Paul's ministry. Why does God's Word have so much power to transform men's lives? Why does it penetrate even to dividing soul and spirit, joints and marrow; and judging the thoughts and attitudes of the heart? Why does it possess so much power of transformation?

God's Word is the Ultimate Truth

In John 17:17, Jesus prayed for God to sanctify His disciples in the truth. And then He said that God's Word is truth. Yes God's Word is the only truth there is. His truth is the cleanest of all truths. It is the only truth by which other truths are measured. In other words, His truth is the standard by which other truths are gaged. His Word is infallible!

Our human understanding of truth has been tainted with the blurry things of this world. It is difficult to find a truthful individual these days. That is one of the reasons our courts are so busy, as lawyers and judges struggle to determine who is telling the truth and who is not. And to worsen an already bad situation, some lawyers sometimes work with the lying party to help them win a case that is based on lies. We find similar occurrences in many of the world's professions, including law enforcement, governments, politics, banking, business and even in the engineering and technical fields.

God's Word is so sharp it cannot be corrupted by these worldly shady practices. That is why it is sharp and straight forward when it penetrates. It separates the truth from lies, often with convictions. God's Word in a person's heart helps him to avoid sin. The Psalmist noted in Psalm 119:11 that he has hid God's Word in his heart so that He might not sin against the Lord. Christians are able to avoid sin because of the knowledge of truth in God's Word.

God's Word Can Never Be Defeated

One of the funniest things on earth is watching the multitudes of unsuccessful attempts that many people and powers have made to bury or overcome the truth. Even very smart people are often humiliated when the truth they are trying to cover up is exposed. The reason is that God's Word (truth) can never be defeated. God's Word is like a live electric wire; hot and full of energy. It tends to show up in one form or the other. When we try to hide the truth, we look like novice children before God who sees everything we do.

Many of the criminal acts that have been solved by the FBI, forensic scientists and other investigators were because the perpetrators made stupid mistakes. This is because, God catches the wise in their craftiness, and the schemes of the wily are swept away (Job 5:13). Moreover, the wisdom of this world is foolishness in God's sight (1Corinthians 3:19). Isaiah 55:10-11 notes that God's Word will not return to Him empty, but will accomplish what He desires and achieve the purpose for which He sent it. His Word is at work in this world. That is one of the reasons we see many of the breakthroughs in the revelations of long-hidden truths in all walks of life. Some examples include folks who have spent many years behind bars being released after it was found out that they were imprisoned by false evidences, hard-core liars and deceivers all of a sudden reversing their original statements after sometime, and thousands of individuals who said that they had to say the truth because they could not live with their guilt.

God's Word has Power

The power of God's spoken Word is seen throughout Jesus' ministry. For example, in Mark 4:35-41, a furious storm came up, and the waves broke over the boat, nearly swamping it. Jesus got up, rebuked the wind and said to the waves to be quiet and be still, and the wind died down and it was completely calm. In Mark 3:1-6, Jesus healed a man with a shriveled hand by telling the man to stretch out his hand. In the book of Acts 3:1-10, the apostle Peter told a lame beggar to rise up and walk in the name of Jesus Christ of Nazareth. Then he took the man by the right hand and helped him up, and instantly the man's feet and ankles became strong and he jumped to his feet and began to walk, to the amazement of all the folks there.

Throughout the Bible, the spoken Word of God is often followed by some form of breakthrough. In Genesis, God spoke the world into existence. The Old Testament prophets and the New Testament apostles all demonstrated the power of God through the spoken Word. In this our dispensation, we experience the power of the spoken Word on a daily basis when we pray in the name of our Lord and Savior Jesus Christ. Prayers are answered on a daily basis in different corners of the globe. Every growing Christian will testify to the fact that prayers are answered on a daily basis. James 5:15 also noted that if Christians are sick, the elders of the church should pray for them and the prayer offered in faith will make the sick person well, and if they have sinned, they will be forgiven.

God's Word is Food

God's Word is our spiritual food. It should be eaten on a regular basis just as ordinary food is eaten three times a day. Just as physical food nourishes and keeps the body healthy, the Word of God nourishes and keeps our spirits healthy and alive. Without constantly eating the Word of God, a person cannot grow in the things of God. The person will be weak, uninformed and prone to satanic manipulations.

In Matthew 4:4, Jesus answered the devil that man shall not live by bread alone, but by every Word that comes from the mouth of God. To know the Word of God, Christians should read the Bible every day, attend Church and other Christian services to fellowship and hear the Word of God preached, and have an altar in their homes where the family can meet, read the Bible, pray and discuss the Word of God together. Reading and learning God's Word does to the soul what milk does to a baby. If a baby is not fed well and on a regular basis, it will not develop well into a fully functioning individual.

It is from this nutritional power of the Word that we gain the knowledge and understanding needed in the work of God which is discussed in the next section. The Word of God impacts knowledge. Through it, we grow in the knowledge of God. In 2 Timothy 2:15, the apostle Paul advised Timothy to study to show himself approved unto God, a workman who did not need to be ashamed, rightly dividing the Word of truth. In Romans 10:17 he declared that faith comes by hearing the Word of God. And in Psalm 119:130, the Psalmist affirmed that the entrance of God's Word gives understanding.

What Christians Can Do with Transformed Lives

The transformative power of God's Word has been discussed above. The purpose of the transformation is to empower Christians to be good instruments for God. God equips His people in the transformation so that they can be usefully involved in His Kingdom. His Kingdom includes this whole wide world.

When Jesus came to introduce Christianity, He stated that when He was lifted up from the earth, He would draw all people to Himself, signifying the nature of His death and the fact that He was a suffering Messiah (John 12:32). And in Mark 16:15-18, he commanded His disciples to go into all the world and preach the Gospel to all creation. He said that whoever believes and is baptized will be saved, but whoever does not believe will be condemned. The Lord was basically calling all His people (believers) to evangelize this whole world. This has been the main task of Christians throughout the ages. All the work of past and future churches, missionaries, evangelists, ministries and Christians has been centered on fulfilling this mission.

What Has Been Accomplished in the Kingdom

When Jesus started to establish His Kingdom, it was just Himself and a handful of the disciples whom He selected. He began with a humble small group who operated in Jerusalem and the Judean countryside, often on foot along the dusty roads of Israel. They operated under the strict and unfriendly Roman rule of their time. And it was also within the wicked reaches and watchful eyes of the Judean Pharisees, High Priests and the Sanhedrin.

Rome used to be anti-Christ and persecuted Christians more than most other societies did. It was a hedonistic society and had many deities in its heydays. But today, the headquarters of the Roman Catholic Church is in Rome. Glory to God.

There are literally millions of churches and Christian schools all over the world today. There are probably as many other Christian fellowships, ministries, colleges and universities, and numerous other Christian groups all over the world. The Bible is still the number one most published and most read book in the whole world. Millions of Christians are ministers and workers in Christianity-related institutions and services all over the world. Christian activities and rituals (prayers, songs, choruses, music, etc.) have permeated most every aspect of the world's social activities, including weddings, funerals, birthdays, graduations, and a host of other parties and events.

Are We There Yet?

Without doubt, the answer is a resounding NO! We are still very far from the goal of evangelizing the whole world. How do we know this?

As of 2013, our world had about 2.2 Billion Christians in it, according to a 2013 World Factbook report. The Factbook estimated the world's population to be about 7,095,217,980 with Christians making about 33.39% of it. Muslims came second with 22.74%, Hindu 13.8%, Buddhist 6.77%, Sikh 0.35%, Jewish 0.22%, and Baha'i 0.11%. Dozens of other religions combined to make up 10.95%, while non-religious folks made up about 9.66%, and atheists about 2.01%.

Although Christians are more in number than other religious and nonreligious groups in world's population, they make up roughly one third the population of the world. This clearly indicates that this as-is Kingdom is hardly half way to its intended destination. There is quite a long way to go in getting that Kingdom to the God who wants all people to be saved and to come to a knowledge of the truth (1 Timothy 2:4). We see Jesus alluding to this in some of His parables and actions. In Matthew 9:36-37, for example, Jesus saw the helpless crowds and had compassion on them. He said that the harvest was plentiful but the workers were few. Our world is full of potential harvests, and we need more Christians to help in the harvests.

How We Can Help to Usher in His Kingdom

The kingdom of God actually begins in us as individuals. As our lives are transformed by the Lord, we become more of Kingdom-bound. Everything about being a participant in God's Kingdom starts with the transformation that took place in our lives. And of course, the Holy Spirit is working in tandem with the transformational work of the Word of God in us at the same time. Surrendering fully to the Lord so that He can fully prepare us takes much prayer, humility, obedience, commitment, action, sacrifice, vision, responsibility and faithfulness.

As our lives are transformed, we find ourselves doing and longing to do many righteous things in the Kingdom. For example, a transformed life will find it easier praying for leaders and those in authority so that we will have peace (1 Timothy 2:1-2) and avoiding evil or living a righteous life in a sinful world. A transformed person should also understand that Christians working in secular workplaces are actually working for God, because:

a) It is all God's Kingdom.

b) He made all things.

c) We are the salt of the Earth.

d) We show examples to the world.

e) His light shines through us.

f) They will not know Him without us.

g) Victorious living is lived in the world.

We can also help to usher in the Kingdom by defeating the enemies in our lives. This is done by shunning sin, by obedience to God's commandments, by becoming best friends with our enemies, by turning evil into good, by making the worst to become the best, by turning hopelessness into hope, by forgiveness, by not judging, and by ministering to the world at the same time. Jesus said to His disciples to proclaim this message: "The kingdom of heaven has come near. Heal the sick, raise the dead, and cleanse those who have leprosy, drive out demons. Freely you have received; freely give" (Matthew 10:7-9). Children of God should try to live like Joshua who said that as for him and his family, they will serve the Lord (Joshua 24:15). They should also live like Caleb who was full of faith and overcame the Anakites or giants that had occupied his territory (Joshua 15:14). We should be living like the salt and light of the world.

What We Can Do to Help Establish His kingdom

Jesus told Peter and other disciples in Luke 4:31-5:11 that He would make them fishers of men. This followed what was clearly an extraordinary event in the lives of His fishermen disciples. Jesus had just preached off the beach using their fishing boat. He had then urged them to move the boat into deeper water and to cast their net into the water. The catch was so much that the nets were breaking. This experience was so much for the disciples that Peter asked Jesus to leave him as he saw himself as a sinner. And it was this experience that promptly cut their fishing career short – they left everything and followed Jesus.

Before this experience, it was said that Jesus went throughout Galilee, teaching in their synagogues, proclaiming the good news of the Kingdom, and healing every disease and sickness among the people (Matthew 4:23). In Acts 10:38, the apostle Peter noted that God anointed Jesus of Nazareth with the Holy Spirit and power, and He went around doing good and healing all who were under the power of the devil, because God was with him. In Hebrew 12:1-2, the author advised us to leave behind everything that hinders us and sin that entangles us from moving forward, but to fix our eyes on Jesus, the Pioneer and Perfecter of our faith.

What these suggestions are pointing to is that Christians should leave behind anything that stops, slows or hinders the progressiveness of the Gospel and focus on the call of the Master to evangelize the world. For example, we should avoid all kinds of sin and focus on the call to righteousness. This is important as sin acts as weight that holds people back from forward mobility. We have seen some of the powerful churches and ministries tumble and fall because of sin. Christians should also try to resolve, overlook or overcome destructive disagreements. We have seen disagreements tear churches, Christian organizations, and friends apart. We must also try not to quit when the going gets tough.

Quitting the fight means no one will do the job that we are entrusted to do.

Our sustained endurance during times of tough situations is of key importance here. Whether it is in sickness, adversary, persecution, hard labor, need or whatever, we should remember that, like soldiers or pilgrims, we have to fight or struggle hard and sustain the impetus before we can completely receive the full reward. Many Christians give in to pressure very easily, forgetting that there is a prize at the end. In this case, the bigger prize is the improvement, increase or good (however little) that will come to the Kingdom. We should never think of that increase as minor, because the cumulative sum of the many little increases is what makes the Kingdom of God great. For example, Jesus started His Kingdom as one individual. He later recruited His disciples, preached and ministered all over His region to build it. Today, His Kingdom has billions of people and is still increasing in size and number.

Above all else, Christians must learn how to love their enemies. The apostle Paul noted that love is patient, kind, does not envy, does not boast, is not proud, does not dishonor others, is not self-seeking, is not easily angered, keeps no record of wrongs, does not delight in evil, rejoices with the truth, always protects, always trusts, always hopes, always perseveres and never fails (1 Corinthian 13). The world is watching Christians at all times. The love we show them makes a whole lot of difference. Many people have been won into the Kingdom because of love. In fact, the topic of love is the subject of the next chapter.

Needed Areas to Minister

Christians have opportunities in just about every part of this world to spread the Gospel. The Gospel is not meant for just folks who come to churches, fellowships and other such religious gatherings. As already mentioned, Jesus went about, teaching, doing good and proclaiming the good news about the Kingdom, and healing every type of disease and sickness among the people. With our world turning into a global village, Christians have greater opportunities to minister everywhere and to everyone. One Christian minister said to Christians to "bloom where they are planted".

The world will know us (Christians) by our love, not by how many churches or facilities we build. Therefore, let us emulate Jesus' style and try to bloom where we are planted. Potential people and areas to reach include folks and coworkers who are non-Christians, tough work environments, schools, neighbors, prisons, friends, networks, clubs, beer parlors, restaurants, movies, hotels, carnivals, picnics, gangs, enemies, court houses and others.

Fighting to Win Vs Fighting to Survive

If you have ever watched two professional boxers fight each other, you would notice that they both usually come out to fight to win. But too often, it is easy to tell which of the two boxers is really fighting to win and which one is just fighting to survive. The battle of the Kingdom is pretty much like that. But the difference is that God has equipped all Christians to fight to win. Christians should know that Christ has overcome the world when he died and rose from the dead. He is with us all the time. Jesus said that all authority in heaven and on earth has been given to Him (Matthew 28:18). Christians must live in prayer to maintain an overcoming lifestyle. The only way a Christian can live a victorious life is to build a life of prayer. Jesus Christ started and ended His days in prayer. Every great man or woman of God spent a good amount of time in prayer. Prayer makes a big difference in a Christian's life.

The apostle Paul also suggested in Romans 14:18 that Christians pray with all kinds of prayer. These include private individual prayers, group or corporate (church or fellowship) prayers, praise, supplication, worship, fasting, casting out demons, prayer of faith, deliverance prayers, praying in the spirit, meditation, and praying while standing up, kneeling down, lying down, walking around, playing instruments and so forth. Whichever works for each person should be exercised daily. Fervent and daily prayerful life unites us with God as friends and team members to one cause. This makes us overcomers and gives us continuous and unbroken series of victories in life. Abraham lived this type of life and was called a friend of God. He and God were so friendly that God said He would not hide His plans from him!

This chapter has discussed the Word of God, including how its power, truth, food and indisputability can transform our lives. It also looked at the various ways we can minister for God after we are transformed through His Word and Holy Spirit. Christians can be most effective when they are equipped by the Word of God. The various areas and opportunities of ministry and how we can approach them are explored. We can be equipped in power, wisdom, knowledge and understanding by learning the Word of God. The next chapter will look into the wonderful love of God for mankind.

Chapter 4

The Deep and Boundless Love, Mercy and Grace of God

The parables of the king and the unforgiving servant (Matthew 18:21-35), and the landowner who went out early in the morning to hire laborers for his vineyard (Matthew 20:1-16), illustrated the deep and boundless love God has for every one of His children in this world. The king in this illustration forgave this servant debtor an amount of money he could not pay, an illustration of the sinful state of mankind and God's wonderful forgiveness of our debts. The landowner was also so generous in paying his hires; he recognized their difficulties in getting hired and decided to pay them all the same irrespective of what time they were hired. This also illustrated the deep and generous love God has for us.

This topic implies that Christians have both expectations and challenges in our walk with the Lord. The first is that we should be encouraged that His love, mercy and grace are ever with us. The second is that we should give the same to others in this world. These will be discussed in more details in the following sections.

The Love, Mercy and Grace of God

Every Christian will attest to the fact that God is generous. He allows His rain and His sun to fall and shine on everyone irrespective of their status in this world. He hears all the prayers of His people and answers all of them according to His will. He is a merciful God and full of compassion for His children. Without His love for mankind, this world would not be around anymore.

Luke 15:11-32 contains the story of the prodigal son who went away and squandered his father's money, but was forgiven by his father upon returning. This again illustrated the deep and boundless love of God for His children. Jesus drove this point home when He told Nicodemus that God loved the world so much that He gave His only begotten Son so that anyone who believes in Him will not perish but have everlasting life (John 3:16).

This story really illustrated the nature of God's love in a way that will help everyone to understand that God loves His creation so dearly and so deeply. It shows that no matter what evil we may have done, He is always longing to see and receive us to Himself when we repent, even when other folks may not want us. Notice that in this story, the prodigal son's brother protested and was against his father's love for the prodigal. Such is the limitation of man that we often are blinded to the fact that it is the love of God that has kept us alive today. We forget the fact that we should show a similar love to our fellow human beings when it is needed.

The Greatest Gift Ever Given

To illustrate His deep and boundless love to His children, God gave us the greatest gift imaginable: His only Son. Can you imagine giving your most precious possession as a gift to someone else? Man's most precious possession is probably our children or something of equal value for folks who have no children. The two notable people who came close to giving their only children to God were Abraham who almost sacrificed his son Isaac to God, and Hannah who gave her son Samuel to Eli the priest for God's service. Even so, Hannah did not sacrifice Samuel.

Also there was the story of a leader by the name of Jephthah who gave his daughter to God in Judges 11:30-39 because of his pledge to God if He gave him victory over Israel's enemies. In fact, it was a common practice in the Old Testament for some people to sacrifice their children to idols, something seen as the ultimate of sacrifices (e.g. Psalms 106:37-38, 2 Chronicles 28:1-3, and 2 Chronicles 33:6). But even so, many of these folks had other children and many of these sacrifices were as a result of some hardship in their lives. These sacrifices cannot be compared to the one and only begotten Son of God who was given for one specific purpose – man's redemption.

Jesus as Man's Hope

Without a person like Jesus, man would not have any hope today. But because of Him, there is salvation for every one of God's children who believes in Him. The apostle Peter put it clearly when he said in Acts 4:12 that salvation is found in no one else, for there is no other name under heaven given to mankind by which we must be saved. Jesus proved to everyone that He was indeed God's gift to the whole world. His virgin birth, sinless life, good deeds, miracles, death and resurrection all attest and point to His divinity. He voluntarily provided Himself and was sacrificed for mankind when we had no other hope. In other words, in our misery, Christ volunteered to take our place. God made Him who had no sin to be sin for us, so that in Him we might become the righteousness of God (2 Corinthians 5:21).

Through Jesus' name, millions and millions of people have reconciled themselves with God. Through His name alone, millions and millions of people have found eternal peace with God. That is why His name is so sweet to millions and millions of folks. He is always in the business of forgiving, cleansing and liberating people from their hopeless situations. When He comes into a life, there is light where darkness used to be. And His blood cleanses us from our sins. He lives forever to continually make atonement for His people. It is said that His love lifted us when nothing else could help.

God's Kind of Love

One may want to know about this special kind of love God has for mankind. Why is God so loving and why is His love so deep and so far reaching? Why is His love difficult for mankind to understand? Why does He love us even when we don't care about Him? Why does He allow some people to continue in their evil deeds without punishing them immediately? And why would He even accept some people to work for Him after all the evil things they committed?

The answer to these questions is that God's kind of love is different from man's kind of love. His kind of love is said to be agape love – an unconditional kind of love, a sacrificial kind of love, an affectionate kind of love, and love that is based on compassion, forgiveness and charity. It is said to be love that truly shows the true nature of God. The apostle John said in 1 John 4:8 that God is love. His love for humans is overwhelmingly deep and generous, and that is why it is difficult for man to understand it. He cares for mankind so much that His love is literally poured out unto man even in his depraved condition.

One way to understand God's generosity is the way He allows His sun and His rain to shine and fall for all. Even if someone was a wicked farmer, God generally allows His rain to fall in the person's farms so that he would grow his crops. His sun and rains help the plants and animals to grow and provide their yields. And everyone, both good and bad, eats of God's yield in order to live and not die.

Another way to illustrate God's love is by the love of a mother for her child. Most mothers would rather go hungry than watch their child go without food. Women are very nurturing and will make sure their children are taken care of. They will go the extra mile to see that their children get what they need to survive. There was the story of one mother who, after jumping out of a burning car, went right back into the car to save her stuck child and ended up perishing with the child in the fire. That is love that knows no bounds.

A Merciful and Gracious God

God's mercy and grace cannot be described either. In the parable of the king and the unforgiving servant discussed in Matthew 18:21-35, the king forgave the servant a big sum of money he could not pay back. The debt was said to be ten thousand bags of gold, something probably in the neighborhood of billions of dollars by today's standard. In this parable, we see mercy and grace working together. It is easy to understand mercy, but grace makes it clear in this story that it took the unmerited favor of this king to forgive this amount of money.

The king in this parable represented God the Father who has so much mercy and grace on His creation. He sees man in his puny, weak condition and knows that without such mercy and grace there is no other way we can ever be free in this world. The big debt represented something we could never have reconciled were it not for the provision made with the blood of Jesus Christ, the Lamb of God. Jesus took our place and died for our sins that we may be reconciled with our God.

In the parable of the landowner who went out early in the morning to hire laborers for his vineyard, discussed in Matthew 20:1, we see the mercy, generosity and grace of God at work. His merciful heart is full of love and he graciously drops it like dew on His children in their difficult situations. This landowner again showed the heart of God in ensuring that everyone is fed (blessed) irrespective of when they were hired. An ordinary heart might not care that some of these men have stood there all day long without being hired. It showed a world system where the haves continue to have more without looking back on the needy. This parable showed the desire of God that all His children will be taken care of.

The Love, Mercy and Grace We Ought to Give to Others

The lessons from the parables of the king and the unforgiving servant will not be complete without looking at the rest of the story. Notice that in the parable of the king and the unforgiving servant, the king had to recall the wicked servant because of what he did to his fellow servant. God expects us to forgive our fellow human beings the way He forgives us. He expects us to be like Him and act like him. That is another secret which every child of God must know. Sometimes, God does not answer our prayers because of this simple reason, and then we wonder why.

The issue of forgiveness is very important to God. In the Lord's Prayer, Jesus prayed for God to "Forgive us our sins even as we forgive others their sins against us". In the parable of the King and the unforgiving servant, we see that requirement illustrated again. There is something about forgiveness that made God to emphasize and require that we give it to others as He gives it to us.

God Expects that We Forgive Others

In the beginning, God made man in His own image (Genesis 1:27). From this information, it can be deduced that God wanted man to have His benevolent qualities, including love, peace, patience, mercy, joy, goodness and forgiveness. From every angle of observation, it just does not seem plausible that God would continue to love mankind who does not love and forgive like Him. And philosophically speaking, it does not seem possible that any of the listed characteristics of God would work for mankind without humans offering forgiveness to fellow humans.

In the Lord's Prayer, Christ clearly stated in Matthew 6:12: "And forgive us our debts, as we also have forgiven our debtors". God fully expects man who was created in His own image to be able to forgive others the way God forgives us all. This is simply His law and expectation and there is no other shortcut to it. When the disciple Peter tried to find if there was a shorter path through this, Jesus told him and others that they should forgive not seven times, but seventy-seven times (Matthew 18:22).

The issue of forgiveness has been a big one for Christians and non-Christians throughout history. It has gotten to a point in our lifetime where it is now used in therapeutic treatments. People of all walks of life are trying to forgive others who have wronged them because of the positive effects of forgiveness. As this book was being written, a mass shooting by a 21-year old, hate-filled young white man took place at Emanuel African Methodist Episcopal Church in downtown Charleston, South Carolina on the evening of June 17, 2015. Nine people were killed, including the senior pastor. The church was one of the United States' oldest black churches and has long been a site for community organization around civil rights. But during the hearing after the young man was apprehended and brought to court, some of the victims' family members expressed their forgiveness of the young shooter.

God Expects that We Show Love, Mercy and Grace to Others

Beyond forgiving other people who have wronged us, the story of the Good Samaritan told in Luke 10:25-37 illustrates how God expects us to treat our neighbors or fellow human beings. This story is full of love, mercy and grace. It also shows that we don't reach our world by religiosity but by God's characteristics of love, mercy and grace.

One of the observations in this story was that the first two people to see the half-dead man were a priest and a Levite, two of the most religious folks of the time. Both men passed by the other side of the road, i.e. they walked away from the side the dying man was lying and walked by on the other side of the road. This is the attitude that showed the half-dead man is filthy, unwanted, dangerous, smelly, unimportant, evil, not God's child, does not need to be helped, not my business or any other reason there is. Many

Christians do this whenever faced with situations they don't want to meddle with.

But the person who stopped to attend to this needy man was a hated Samaritan. This Samaritan took pity on him, went to him, bandaged his wounds, poured on oil and wine, put the man on his own donkey, brought him to an inn, took care of him, took out and gave the innkeeper two denarii to look after him and promised to reimburse for any extra expense they may have made when he returned. Jesus explained that the person who was a neighbor to this sick man was the Samaritan and that we should go and do likewise.

It is difficult to look at this story and not look at our lives as Christians, especially in relation to our work of spreading the Gospel. The simple truth from this story is that no amount of religiosity, doctrine or ceremony will help to draw the dying world to the Kingdom of God more than Christians putting on the simple characters of God such as love, mercy, grace and forgiveness. The main thing a dying, sick or hungry person needs is how to survive. Often, salvation of the soul follows humanitarian gestures.

Implications for Christians: The apostle John advised Christians in John 4:7 to love one another, for love is from God and everyone who loves is born of God and knows God. Love cannot be consummated without God's kind of forgiveness. And the fullness of love comes when we have forgiveness, mercy, grace and other characteristics of God in us. This embodiment has great benefits for every child of God.

For one, and perhaps the biggest, the Kingdom of God is fostered and expanded – thus meeting His purpose. This will make the Father very happy about us. Secondly, we have many personal benefits including health benefits. Doctors and folks in the health and medical fields appear to be telling us that a forgiving attitude helps the body to function better. It is better to live a life of forgiveness than to live with hate. A hateful heart has more tendency to be sad than a free one. Another strong point to make here is that of delayed or unanswered prayers. Christians should do their best to forgive others, as well as wear all other God's characteristics to ensure they are in tune with the Lord. It is His commandment that we forgive others even as He forgives us. James 4:6 says that God opposes the proud but shows favor to the humble. Last but not the least, our world gets better as we forgive. Both the forgiver and the forgiven live in a happier, more peaceful world. Plus the forgiven may often change their lives for good.

This chapter discussed the deep and boundless love, mercy and grace of God. It looked at Jesus as man's hope, and examined God's kind of love. It also discussed the love, mercy and grace we ought to give to others. Then it examined why God expects that we forgive others and why He expects that we show love, mercy and grace to them. The implications for Christians were also discussed. The next chapter will discuss the responsibility, preparedness and accountability that God expects of His children.

CHAPTER 5

The Responsibility, Preparedness and Accountability that God Expects of His Children

The characteristics of responsibility, preparedness and accountability are treated together in this section because of their relatedness and their complementary nature. It is difficult to discuss one without the other. The three are very important to the Kingdom of God. He expects all His children to be wise, accountable and responsible. Like the case of responsibility, He will hold His children accountable for every talent and assignment that are entrusted to them. While not every one of God's children has the same degree of responsibility, some people are utterly irresponsible in some key areas of life. In the case of the ten virgins, it is said that the five foolish ones took their lamps but did not take any oil with them. But the five wise ones took oil in jars along with their lamps. When the groom finally arrived at mid night, the virgins who were ready went in with him to the wedding banquet while the other five who were not ready were not allowed to attend (Matthew 25:1-13). There is evidence of unpreparedness and irresponsibility in this story. In the parable of the sower which Jesus told in Matthew 13:3-9, the seed could not germinate in the unprepared soil but germinated in the good soil. This story showed the need for mankind to prepare his heart for the Word of God to germinate and grow in it.

In the parable of the king who prepared a great wedding for his son narrated in Matthew 22:1-14, there is ample evidence that the king painstakingly prepared a feast for folks who did not care about him and his business. It sounded more like God wasting His time preparing beautiful riches for people in this world who have no time or interest for him and His Kingdom. Clearly, this is utter irresponsibility and unpreparedness on man's part. In the parable of the talents, while two of the servants performed according to their abilities, one of the servants buried his master's talent and did not produce any profit with it. Again, there is evidence of irresponsibility on the part of this one servant who buried his master's talent. As a result of this, his master said to cast the worthless servant into the outer darkness where there would be weeping and gnashing of teeth (Matthew 25:14-30).

Responsibility

The key to the responsibility expectation from God is found in the nature of His assignments to us. Responsibility relates to a person's duty, charge or obligation as a Christian with respect to the gift and calling God has given to him or her. It follows the individual to every level of life, including personal, family, community, career and professional obligations. Responsibility can be something as simple as dressing one's bed in the morning, brushing one's teeth, or keeping one's house/apartment or car cleaned, to any of the many higher roles in life like being the teacher, manager, director or president of a class, company, city or country. In the same token, God expects Christians to be responsibly prepared for any occasion that involves His Kingdom. Responsibility here can be looked at from two perspectives, namely: responsibility as a gift or talent, and responsibility as a commitment.

Responsibility as a Gift or Talent

The first perspective of responsibility is the assignment God the Father has assigned to each of us. Every one of God's children has a responsibility assigned to them. This is represented by the talents in the parable of the man who gave talents to his servants. This master expected his servants to be responsible investors with their assigned talents. In the same token, God expects all His children to be productive with the gifts He has given them. In this perspective, responsibility is seen as a gift.

Every human created by God has one or more gifts or talents. These gifts can be expressed through mental abilities, creativity, philosophies, physical abilities, intelligence and so forth. Some are more pronounced than others. And some people show their gifts in more remarkable ways than others. For example, many of the world's Noble Laureates are gifted in the arts, sciences etc. Likewise, many artists, musicians and sports stars are gifted. There are designers, singers, leaders, teachers, writers, boxers, counselors, chefs, actors, engineers, dancers, preachers, students, and doctors who are exceptionally more gifted or talented in their trades because of this. Therefore, while many people can train to qualify to perform different trades and occupations, the fact remains that there are folks who are gifted in those same trades and they show it through their exemplary workmanship.

Moreover, God's gifts can be improved through training and practice. King David was a notable example who, through the training he undertook while working as a shepherd boy, learned (1) how to play his musical instrument so well that he would later be employed to play for King Saul to sooth his torments, (2) how to compose many songs used to worship the Lord in the land of Israel, and which are still being used today all over the world, (3) how to shoot a stone from a sling so well he could hit a giant by the name of Goliath in the forehead, thus bringing a great victory to Israel, and (4) how to lead the sheep so well that he was able to lead God's people better than other kings.

Most of the gifted people in the world today spend significant amounts of time practicing their gifts to help them improve. Musicians practice and audition a lot to perfect their acts before their appearances. Professional basketball players practice for hours to improve in their skills before their tournaments. In the same token, God expects us to train and practice on our skills, talents or gifts so that we will improve and become perfected in order to do a good job for Him and be more productive. In 2 Timothy 2:15, Paul advised Timothy to do his best to present himself to God as one approved, a worker who does not need to be ashamed and who correctly handles the Word of truth.

Responsibility as a Commitment

The second perspective of responsibility is the way we carry out the assignments of God. In this, like in just about any type of assignment, some Christians are more responsible than others. Sometimes, this is expressed as being more productive, more resourceful, more committed or attentive than others. This type of responsibility can be measured by examining the results.

Finally, it must be emphasized here that responsibility can be measured by judgment or by quantification. For example, supervisors and managers in workplaces can determine whether their workers' accomplishments for the day, week, month, year, or the period of the review were poor, satisfactory, very good or excellent. They can also determine that quantitatively, based on simple fractions or percentages. Note that the tasks can be just about anything, skilled or unskilled, managerial or technical. It does not matter what the nature of the job is; once it is measured, a supervisor can easily determine the proportion that was accomplished, and then make his or her decision based on that proportion. This explains why some employees progress more than others in earning promotions, awards, leadership positions, and such likes. Organizations have different ways of rewarding their employees on their achievements. These employees' accomplishments are determined in much the same way as measurement of their responsibility.

From the foregoing discussions on responsibility measurement, it is clear that one's degree of responsibility can be easily determined by the all-knowing God. If ordinary managers and supervisors can determine workers' accomplishments, how much better could our God who made heaven and earth do that?

Preparedness

Spiritual readiness is key in successful Christian living. Living here means in everything God has called us to do in life. Some of our roles in which we have to be prepared include our homes, neighborhoods, workplaces, churches and communities. It is also a mark of obedience to the Lord when we are consistent in loving Him. In this characteristic, the Lord wants us to be prepared in two ways. Understanding what these characteristics mean and how they relate to our lives will help us to live a more holy and acceptable life for the Master.

Ever-ready Preparedness

The first preparation is for each servant to be rapturable. Christians ought to be ready to welcome the Lord any time He appears to take His people home. Jesus said that His coming will be as unexpected as when a thief comes to steal in the night. If His coming to take His people home is going to be so unannounced, then it behooves every Christian to be prepared for such a sudden departure from this earth.

This kind of departure can either be when He shows up for rapture, or when a Christian dies or departs from this world. No person really knows what date and hour they are going to die. Today, some folks die by accidents, while some die by diseases or natural causes. Some die by suicide, assassination, or execution for their crimes. No one really knows how he or she is going to die. Therefore, the best thing every person should do is to make sure that they are prepared before their time.

Preparation here means to be ready as in ever-ready. God wants us to be ready for heaven at any time. It is not like folks who commit sins today and hope to ask for God's forgiveness tomorrow. Take the case of a man who died but, because of temptation, had been involved in an armed robbery the previous week. He was intending to ask God for forgiveness, but could not do it in time before he died. Or take the case of a man who owed a business man a substantial amount of money, so big that the businessman was literally whimpering in his business as a result. In spite of repeated efforts to get this debtor to pay the debt, it was never paid until the debtor died. Consequently, the business man lost his business and his health, while his family of eight children suffered terribly. I wonder what this debtor would tell God when he got to heaven, since he had the opportunity to pay this debt and refused to pay it while he could.

These kinds of sad stories can be avoided if God's children are prepared in their daily duties. We should be sensitive to God's commandments. We should do our best to avoid sin in all its forms. We should be sensitive to the voice of the Lord, knowing that He sees everything we do. When we make a mistake and fall into sin, we must repent and ask for forgiveness immediately. Postponing our repentance only shows that we are not serious with His commandments.

Preparedness in His Service

The other type of preparedness relates to the assignments or services we do for Him. This is more of how careful we approach such assignments. The Lord illustrated this in Matthew 24:45-51 where the faithful servant carefully maintained his assignment much to the delight of his master. The unfaithful servant, on the other hand, spent his time carelessly and even beat up his fellow servants. Jesus said that the master of that servant would come on a day and at an hour when he did not expect him, and would cut him to pieces and assign him a place with the hypocrites, where there would be weeping and gnashing of teeth.

To prepare for this type of service, we should be meticulous to the call of duty and meticulous to the details of the assignment. We may need to learn the pros and cons of the assignment so that we can perform it well to the Master's satisfaction. A satisfactory service to Him will cause Him to say "Thou faithful and wise servant". This is the most satisfying acknowledgement or blessing any Christian can receive from the Lord. There was an event that happened in a household where the mistress had three maids. One of the maids was wiser than the other two. She knew that the most effective way of winning their mistress' favor was by carefully taking good care of her four children. So she would give them a good birth, wash their clothes, feed them well, and keep close watch on them without having their mistress demand that. She made sure to play with the children and never spanked or talked hard to them. As a result, all the kids took her as if she was a mother to them. Their mother liked her more than the other maids. She also gave her more access to food and other leadership privileges in the house.

One way to please God with our preparedness is to avoid the so-called eye service. Eye service means serving the Master only when He is looking or when people are seeing us perform the service. We should know that God cannot be mocked by man. He is Spirit and sees in the same realm. He knows our thoughts and intents. He is all knowing. He demands truth in the innermost being. Therefore, it is in our best interest to serve Him with constancy of purpose. We should not worry about whether anyone sees us or not. Our God is a Rewarder of those who worship Him in spirit and in truth.

The story of Cornelius is a popular one in the Bible (Acts 10). He gave arms (gifts) to the needy and did many other good deeds. It is not clear whether this man was a "Christian" or not, but the fact that he was devout, feared God, and did good things prompted God to send Peter to preach the Gospel to him. In the process of Peter and his associates doing this duty, the man and all the people with him received the Holy Spirit as well. This man received more than he had expected. It is no secret that when we please God, He often pays back in a bigger way than we expected. Too often, He does these things when we don't expect them.

Are Some Christians Abusing Their Office?: Much of what is happening in the churches and other Christian organizations today indicate that serious violations are taking place in many of these institutions. These violations have become so common that many non-Christians and Christians do not take the Church as a serious institution anymore. There have been cases of deception, sexual abuse of minors, mismanagement of money, and so many others.

These issues should not be happening in the Church, the one symbol that represents Christianity in the world today. How can these managers stand before the Lord when they meet Him to give account of their work? How can they justify these evils when they consider their negative and disastrous consequences to the Church?

For one, these sins are not helping the Kingdom of God. They are hindering the work of God and bringing a bad image to the Church. They are also damaging the faith of many Christians, to say the least. The Lord said that anyone who causes the least of His children to err would be better off drowning in the depths of the sea with a large millstone hung around their neck (Matthew 18:6). The Lord's work demands care and purity. We must do it with holiness. We must remove selfishness from it. Only God will get the glory. Anything that pollutes His Kingdom or stands in the way of achieving it will be cursed.

The parable of the sower and the parable of the king who prepared a great wedding for his son both illustrated God's expectations of anyone who wants to partake in His riches. His Word is our spiritual food, and to be invited to His banquet is a great honor to mankind. In each of these cases, we must show ourselves prepared.

Being prepared here involves much care. The term "care" means being careful in one's life to avoid sinful things like stubbornness, pride, worldliness, neglect, omissions, forgetfulness, selfishness, mistakes and other every day sins. Just about every successful Christian is known to possess this quality. A careful Christian is very meticulous in carrying out God-related responsibilities. Although no Christian is perfect, but careful ones tend to have fewer of these costly preparedness problems. Notice that in the case of the sower, the seed germinated and bloomed only in the prepared or ready soil but did not do well on the rocky, thorny and hard ones. In the case of the king who prepared a wedding banquet, he did his best to bring all the invitees, but they paid no attention and went off—one to his field, another to his business, while the rest seized his servants and mistreated and killed them. Even when he authorized his servants to go into the street corners and invite everyone they could find, he still noticed a man among them in the banquet who was not wearing wedding clothes. In other words, this man was not prepared for the banquet.

One of the main reasons God wants us to be prepared at all times is so we cannot be denied of any of His blessings. One Christian was earnestly privately praying for another Christian man to be healed late one night. He wondered why God would allow this brother to suffer such a serious illness in spite of the fact that he was into God's service. As he meditated on the situation, the following information involving the man he was praying for and another rich friend of his was revealed to him. The information was in the form of a question: "Why should I heal (or help) someone who would steal his government's (or people's) money and use it on himself? Why should I heal someone who is so disrespectful to others by lording over others to get his way?"

Yes, preparedness means Christians being ready when the Lord returns. Jesus said that He would come back again. He clearly said it in John 13:3 when He said that He was going to prepare a place for us, and that He would come back and take us to be with Him that we also may be where He is. Now the question is: Will He find us ready or not? We must be prepared by living a righteous life, a life that pleases God. We must be ready at all times, and that readiness demands that we always maintain a holy living, for without holiness no one will see Him.

Accountability

Accountability is the last frontier in the gifts God gave to His children. It is defined as giving account of what someone did with something of value given to him or her. In the business world, it is sometimes referred to as taking stock. It is usually performed at the end of a quarter, term or year depending on what type of period the business is using.

In the Kingdom of God, accountability focuses on two key things: what we did with our talents or gifts, and what we did with our lives. The parable of the talents made it clear that these two areas of accountability will be required of every one on the last day. There is a lot of theology around these topics, but it will be made clear in this book that it will be difficult or impossible to achieve the former without the later. The reason for this is that to be rewarded for any good work, the person has to be born again first and the good work should be something that glorifies the Lord in His Kingdom. Some talented people are not born-again Christians, and they do their work for causes other than the Kingdom of God. For example, there are some talents that basically encourage evil in the Kingdom of God. Paul warned that idolaters, drunkards, revelers, and people who do such things cannot see the Kingdom of God. There are folks who perform their talents just to be praised and to enrich themselves instead of the Kingdom of God. There are those who encourage young people to use illegal drugs, disobey their parents and authorities, and participate in wild, worldly, and godless activities.

When people are born again, they fear God and do decent work that gives glory and honor to God. There was a former born-again United States' President who spent hundreds of hours of his time helping to teach Sunday school classes, construct homes for poor folks and so many other similar things. There was a highly successful born-again boxer who helped many of his countrymen and later served in his county's legislature. There are millions of born-again Christians who honor God with their lives in multitudes of places and in every corner of the world today. These are the folks who may receive a good reward on the account of their lives at the end of the journey. The Bible clearly indicated that everyone must give account of his or her life to God. This is referring to whether we lived a godly life and whether we are born again. In other words, we must give account about how we lived in God's Kingdom.

In 1 Cor. 3:11-14 and Revelations 22:12, it is suggested that everyone will receive a reward for how they ran their race. In this judgement, Christians who are more faithful than others will receive special rewards for their service to the Lord. Some Christians will receive more than others because of their higher calling and heavier dedication to the work in the Kingdom. However, only God knows those people and what each person will receive. He sees the heart, the intent and efforts of each Christian. It is certain that He rewards accountability and preparedness of His children. In the case of the ten virgins, the five wise virgins enjoyed the banquet. In the case of the talents, the two productive servants were praised and promoted to manage a larger share. They were also told to enter into the joy of their master. This helps to explain why some people are not happy in this world. The simple answer is that we must make the Master happy before we can enjoy our own happiness.

Also, embedded in the parable of the talents is the fact that God has given certain talents as gifts to His children. These gifts are given in certain measures. In other words, they are given to God's children according to our various abilities. Thus, some Christians who have more abilities than others may receive more of these gifts than others. However, getting more or bigger gift than others does not necessarily mean that the person is more important than others. It simply means that those individuals have greater abilities to manage greater responsibilities than others.

This chapter has examined the significance and the ramifications of the important topics of responsibility, preparedness and accountability in the Kingdom of God.

It is clear from their ramifications that God expects every one of His children to be well-rounded and well equipped in these key valuable characteristics of His Kingdom in order to be a useful and productive child to Him. The next chapter will discuss why our presence on earth is referred to as living among the non-Christians of the world.

Chapter 6

God's Children Living Amongst the Non-Christians of the World

The parable of the weed and the parable of the dragnet discussed in Matthew 12:24-52 and Matthew 13:47 both illustrate the fact that God's children live with people of the world who do not necessarily like them. They also illustrate the struggles that Christians experience when living among folks who do not share their values. There is bound to be strife, hatred, persecutions and all sorts of unpleasant experiences. Weed is found almost everywhere good food crop is planted. Farmers do not burn them up with the good crops, but must carefully uproot and destroy them to protect their food crops. In the parable of the weed, the farmer wanted to separate the weed from the good crops during his harvest time. In the case of the dragnet, however, a dragnet was cast into the sea and gathered both good and bad sea creatures. When the net was full, the fishermen drew it to the shore and gathered the good ones into vessels, but threw the bad ones away. Again, there is cohabitation of the good and bad sea creatures in this story.

In my book titled *"A Table Prepared Before Me"*, I did an extensive discussion on why it is necessary for God's children to live in this kind of arrangement. The weed and bad sea creatures in these parables literally mean enemies who do not bring anything of value to the table. In terms of everyday living, enemies are many and varied. They vary in powers, ranks and authorities. They are found at every level of society, including families, organizations, local, state, national and international communities. While enemies are found at varied entities, enemies are people and spiritual powers that work for Satan. Although many of these people do not know that they are being used by Satan, their actions are against the children of God. In other words, they work against the will of God. Whether they know it or not, they are basically agents of Satan. Our enemies are many and can be grouped into three major categories, including fellow humans, demons, and Satan himself.

However, there are very strong reasons why God allowed this cohabitation to happen. The reasons include the following: there is only one earth; we need to be cleansed as well; the world is our training camp; we need experience; it is a great opportunity to exercise our faith; and we need to make disciples. These reasons are not exhaustive, but will provide enough answers to help Christians understand why they are in the fight.

There is Only One Earth

We have to live on earth with everyone including our enemies. There is only one earth and we must share it together. That means working with everyone including friends and foes, studying with them, attending functions with them, making decisions with them, and sometimes getting in relationships with them.

We Need to be Cleansed for the Kingdom of God

We Christians need to be cleansed of our own personal and individual garbage through the baptism of the fire which John the Baptist alluded to in Matthew 3:11-12. What better way to cleanse us of our junks than to place us in a real life environment. No other experience can prepare a person better than learning on the job. Even employers know that the more experience applicants have the more useful they will become to the company hiring them. Another way to put it is what the Lord referred to as being pruned. He is the Vine and we are the branches. God prunes us so that we can bear more fruits. Persecutions, trials and problems have a way of launching Christians to higher levels in life. Fiery trials of enemy oppression help to toughen a child of God. This is often accompanied by significant spiritual growth and more ability to face bigger issues in the future.

It should be noted that without this cleansing, Christians will be living a life of drag in which there is really no victory and not much joy in their lives. The apostle Paul put it this way in Hebrews 12:1: "Therefore, since we are surrounded by such a great cloud of witnesses, let us throw off everything that hinders and the sin that so easily entangles. And let us run with perseverance the race marked out for us…" Many Christians still have issues that need to be dealt with, and the various situations we encounter in this world provide opportunities for curing us of those issues. Some examples are:

- Uncontrollable anger
- Lack of self-control
- Disrespect for authorities and others
- Theft or stealing what does not belong to a person
- Laziness
- Hatred
- Unfaithfulness
- Uncaring attitude
- Selfishness
- Stubbornness
- Overeating and/or over drinking
- Unfairness
- Ignorance
- Disobedience or rebellion
- Sexual sins like adultery, fornication, pornography and other forms of sexual immoralities
- Idolatry
- Covetousness
- Discord
- Unforgiveness
- Greed
- Irresponsibility
- Telling lies

True joy and victory come when all the unnecessary weights of sin are offloaded from us. We are cleansed when we humble ourselves, examine ourselves, and allow the Holy Spirit to help us shed everything we carry that is not pleasing to God. These weights can be in the form of what we eat (like drugs, junks, hard liquors, and toxins), what we say (cursing, insults, foolish words, and careless words), where we go (bad clubs, joints, and ungodly places), what we look at (pornography, violence, immorality, and torture), and what we think or do (drunkenness, cheating, lying, stealing, hating, abusing, fighting, and other reckless behaviors).

The World is Our Training Camp

Related to the above discussions on our need for personal cleansing is the fact that we are in a training camp. David went through the camp of shepherding his father's sheep where he learned the skill of killing lions and bears, to become the strong man who killed Goliath, an event that launched him into a new elevation in history. Every human being, whether Christian or non-Christian, must undergo the experiences of this world which no other training camp can provide. For Christians, it is a great opportunity that will help us to be sharpened, pruned, tried, taught, heat-treated, tempered, hardened, worked and smoothed into beautiful gems for the Master.

And so brothers and sisters, consider your situation of the moment a training camp. The experiences you garner now will culminate in the mighty victories of tomorrow. Killing lions and bears are not fun experiences. The experiences at this level are for the most part terrorizing and uninviting.

Sometimes, they can be life-threatening, but one day the ultimate result will be an event or events that bring much joy. Consider it pure joy whenever you face trials of many kinds, because the testing of your faith develops perseverance. And perseverance must finish its work so that you may be mature and complete, not lacking anything (James 1:2-4).

We Need Experience for the Kingdom of God

Christians need to have these experiences in order to grow and mature. Growth and maturity mean we can be stronger and good enough to help and encourage other struggling Pilgrims so we can become "perfected". Otherwise, how can we help someone with a splinter in their eye when we have a log in ours?

It is a Great Opportunity to Exercise Our Faith

Hebrews chapter 11 has a litany of men and women of faith who accomplished great things through their great faith in God. All these accomplishments took place in this world, not in heaven. It will not be possible for children of God to overcome hardship (and thus grow) if they do not have the kinds of challenges that only this world's problems can bring. It is an awesome opportunity for Christians to step out like their older brothers and sisters and accomplish the same things these days for the glory of God.

In Hebrews 12:2-3, the apostle Paul instructed that we should fix our eyes on Jesus, the Author and Perfecter of our faith, who for the joy set before Him endured the cross, scorning its shame, and sat down at the right hand of the throne of God. We should consider Him who endured such opposition from sinful men, so that we will not grow weary and lose heart. The Lord Jesus left for us a perfect example of how to live in this world. We should be courageous, righteous, humble, and focus our sight on the prize. The table He has prepared for us is for His glory. It will be difficult for the enemies in this world to stop our efforts if we work with this type of approach.

We Need to Make Disciples for the Kingdom of God

We have to make disciples from our enemies. Living away from them and not intermingling with them gives us no opportunity to do this. Christ said that a man's own enemies would be members of his household (Matthew 10:36). Even though we live in a very wicked world, we are designed to love our enemies in such a way that they become friends with us.

Many Christians today are folks who used to hate their Christian neighbors. But through the work of the Holy Spirit, these have been converted to become some of the best friends with the very people they once hated. The power of God overcomes any type of wall that the enemy may erect. Stephen loved and prayed for his executioners while he was being stoned to death. As a result, the Gospel spread to many areas, and many non-Christians became Christians out of all that hate-inspired act. One of those that emerged to become a great Christian was the apostle Paul who later wrote one of the best chapters on love (1 Corinthians 13).

Moreover, Christians often need to be restored and sharpened. No Christian is without sin and mistakes. We need repentance and forgiveness. Living and working with our enemies is an enormous opportunity to become better Christians, in restoring our relationships with God and in finding His perfect will for us. Often repentance brings newer visions and opportunities for reaching the world for Christ. King David recognized this after committing adultery with Bathsheba and murdering her husband. David prayed God to "Restore to me the joy of your salvation and grant me a willing spirit to sustain me. Then I will teach transgressors your ways, so that sinners will turn back to you" (Psalm 51:12-13).

The Challenge of Long Waiting Times

It is not exaggerating to say that most prayer requests by Christians take some amount of time to be answered. While some prayers take shorter times to be answered, some prayers take longer times before they are answered. For some Christians, the waiting can be unusually long, sometimes lasting for years on end. In Matthew 8:5-14, Jesus instantly healed a centurion's servant and Peter's mother-in-law. In the servant's case, Jesus simply spoke the word from a remote location and the servant was healed. In the case of Peter's mother-in-law, Jesus went to the house and touched her hand. David waited for years from the time Samuel anointed him as king of Israel to the time he actually became the king of Israel. Much of that time he was running for his life as his master King Saul was constantly hunting for him to be killed. The father of faith (Abraham) waited a life time without actually seeing the promise (that he would be the father of nations) materialize. And yet, it happened.

Therefore, the key component of a prayer life in our type of challenging world is faith that our request will be answered. Every Christian must have faith. Without faith, it is impossible to please God (Hebrews 11:6). While God will always answer His children, we need to know that faith and time go together. Clearly, some prayers take shorter lengths of time to be answered, but some take longer lengths of time before we see them answered. We tend to be more concerned about the ones that take longer lengths of time to be answered. Sometimes, some Christians tend to give up or lose hope after waiting for a while. What many Christians don't realize is that God has reasons for the waiting process. He is the all-knowing Father and will not allow us to have something at the wrong time or to have something we truly don't need. There are so many mysteries behind this issue that an exhaustive discussion of it cannot be completed in a book of this size. But it should be enough to know that there are some reasons why we have to wait longer sometimes before our prayers can be answered. One good example is found in the story of the Jewish people.

The Jews had to live in Egypt for over 400 years in order to reach a population that formed a great army large enough to face mighty nations. But the process of growing that mighty army was never sweet – it was mixed with torture, suffering, and much waiting. Even when their deliverer Moses finally showed up, the suffering had reached to a point where new Jewish baby boys had to be killed. But the Bible said that when Balak the king of Moab and his people saw all that

Israel had done to the Amorites, they were terrified because there were so many Israelites. Indeed, Moab was filled with dread because of the Israelites (Numbers 22:2). The psalmist alluded to this in Psalm 105:24 when he said that "The Lord made his people very fruitful; He made them too numerous for their foes." God multiplied the people of Israel until they became too mighty for their enemies. But it took over 400 years to be accomplished.

Godly waiting almost always results in benefits for the waiters. Although the waiting process can be torturously painful and tormenting sometimes, good things often happen during and/or after the period of the waiting. Sampson's hair was growing while the Philistines kept him in prison, so long that by the time they decided to bring him out to perform for them, he had regained so much of his strength to be able to kill so many of them, more than his combined kill during his entire life as Israel's judge (Judges 16:23-30).

Nothing tests the Christian's faith more than longer waiting times. God knows the things He wants to accomplish in our lives during the waiting process. James 1:2-4 tells us that the testing of our faith produces perseverance. The only way to strengthen one's muscles is by exercising and bearing load. The muscles often get sore during such exercise. There are no short cuts to getting stronger unless we face some resistance. As more and more weights are added to the bar, the muscles scream because they are sore; but they get stronger in the process. The waiting process produces similar results in Christians. As we wait, more knowledge is gained, our wisdom is expanded, we get stronger in the Lord, we grow in our spiritual life, and more unknown mysteries (like in the case of Sampson's hair) are developed. While we may not understand it during the waiting process, one thing is sure: we will be very happy in the end. And it also results in better and increased benefits to the Kingdom of God.

This chapter has discussed the parables of the weed and the dragnet, and examined their implications for God's children who live amongst the non-Christians of this world. As children of God who work in His Kingdom, a lot is at stake for the Kingdom and for Christians. There are many reasons why we must cohabit with non-Christians in this world. The reasons include the fact that there is only one earth, we need to be cleansed for the Kingdom of God, the world is our training camp, we need to gain experience for the Kingdom of God, it is a great opportunity to exercise our faith, and we need to make disciples for the Kingdom of God. The next chapter will discuss some other important characteristics of the Kingdom of God.

Chapter 7

Other Characteristics of the Kingdom of God

While some of the characteristics discussed here are actually embedded in the parables of the Kingdom and in the previous chapters already discussed, a few are selected here to provide a richer supplement to the discussions of the characteristics of the Kingdom of God. God's Kingdom is full of rich values. Therefore, a comprehensive discussion of it should include these important characteristics which are evident throughout His Kingdom.

The Kingdom of God is so broad that its characteristics beggar description. Even ordinary earthly kings and leaders often appear too much for mankind to describe. Consider the case of King Solomon who was described as the wisest and richest man that has ever lived on planet earth. It was said of his wisdom that other kings either visited him or sent their representatives to Jerusalem to witness his wisdom. His daily provisions alone were said to be some 5.5 tons of the finest flour, 11 tons of meal, 10 stall-fed cattle, 20 pasture-fed cattle, 100 sheep and goats, as well as deer, gazelles, roebucks and choice fowl (1 Kings 4:22-24). Similar things can be said about some presidents of some rich and powerful nations of our modern time. For example, when the President of the United States says something, the world usually takes note of it. And just about every young person from every part of the world likes to live in the United States because of its economic status, opportunities and freedom.

If the above characteristics can be attributed to ordinary earthly leaders and their kingdoms, what shall we say about other characteristics of God's Kingdom? The answer is there are still many other bigger and better characteristics of God's Kingdom. However, just a few of them will be discussed here because of the sheer number of His Kingdom's characteristics. The fact is that God's Kingdom can never be compared with any earthly kingdom because His Kingdom is just too much for man to comprehend.

Miracles

Some glimpses of God's Kingdom were actually revealed by Jesus Christ Himself and are still ever present in our midst today. Some of them are the performances and occurrences of miracles, events that can only take place by Divine means. While miracles have been performed by some Old Testament prophets, Jesus made them rather more personal as things God's children could do if they only have faith in Him. Take the case of what happened in Matthew 17:14-21 for an example. Jesus just healed a man that had seizures, a man His disciples could not heal. When His disciples asked

Him why they couldn't drive it out, Jesus replied that it was because they had so little faith. He also stated that if they had faith as small as a mustard seed, they could say to any mountain to move from here to there and it would move, and nothing would be impossible to them.

We see similar miracles happening in many Christian circles. Most Christians who have been delivered from different difficult situations can testify of the various miraculous ways God helped them to pull out and become free and successful. We see these in testimonies of healings, successful careers, marriage and family restorations, miracle babies, academic achievements, deliverances from catastrophic accidents, and the list can go on and on. But the key thing is to have faith in God. Christians should never overlook the possibility and availability of miracles in the Kingdom of God.

Progress

Another characteristic of the Kingdom of God is the tendency of godly people to grow. Growth here means to be successful in life – wisdom, knowledge, abilities, riches and well-being. It is God's intent that His children prosper like Abraham. In 3 John 1:2, the apostle John wrote that he wished above all things that his fellow Christians would prosper and be in health even as their souls prospered. The psalmist blessed the Lord in Psalm 103:3-5 for forgiving him all his iniquities, healing all his diseases, redeeming his life from destruction, crowning him with lovingkindness and tender mercies, and for satisfying his mouth with good things so that his youth was renewed like the eagle's. In Psalm 92:12-13, he declared that the righteous will flourish like a palm tree, and that they will grow like a cedar of Lebanon. And planted in the house of the Lord, the righteous will flourish in the courts of our God. In Psalm 128:1-4, he declared that all who fear the Lord and who walk in obedience to Him are blessed. He said that they will eat the fruit of their labor and that blessings and prosperity will be their lot. The wives of people who fear the Lord will be like a fruitful vine within their homes, and their children will be like olive shoots around their tables. In Luke 6:38, the Lord Jesus admonished us that if we give gifts to others, it will not only be given to us, but it will be poured into our laps in good measure, pressed down, shaken together and running over.

God's children are supposed to be doing well in everything they engage. While they live in an imperfect world and endure all the trials and tribulations of this world, in the end all things work together for them because they love God (Romans 8:28). As long as they remain steadfast in the Lord and do His will, their lives will be blessed. The Bible is replete with men and women who were blessed because of this simple rule. Great examples included folks like Abraham, Joseph, Hannah, David, Daniel, Esther and Mary, just to name a few.

Peace

Not only is peace a characteristic feature of God's Kingdom, peace is also something that is sought in every kingdom. The apostle Paul wrote that the peace of God which passes all understanding shall keep our minds in Christ Jesus (Philippians 4:7). Jesus is the Prince of peace. Therefore His Kingdom is peaceful and all His subjects shall have peace.

God's peace passes all understanding. His peace is not like world's peace. His peace is ever present in spite of circumstances people face every day in this world. Paul talked about this peace in Philippians 4:7 when he said that the peace of God, which transcends all understanding would guard the Philippian Christians' hearts and minds in Christ Jesus. This is the kind of peace that people need to navigate this world today.

This world is not a peaceful place. Tragedies and all sorts of evils happen in it every day. There are wars, floods, fires, earthquakes, violence, sicknesses and diseases, divorces, quarrels, armed robberies, accidents, job losses, poverty and a host of other social, political and economic problems surrounding mankind today. This world will promise only temporary or artificial short-term fixes. We see world leaders attending one global conference after another trying to fix one issue or the other. By the time one war is settled, several other wars have already started around the globe and thousands of innocent lives are lost in the process. How can God's people maintain their peace in spite of all these ills?

The answer is found only in the Kingdom of God. Paul alluded to this when he wrote that God's Kingdom is not a matter of eating and drinking, but of righteousness, peace and joy in the Holy Spirit (Romans 14:17). In Matthew 11:28, Jesus beckoned all who are weary and burdened to come to Him, and He would give them rest. He is the Author of peace. He is the Prince of peace. His peace is not of this world. The story of how Jesus calmed a furious storm that had sent the waves over his boat is a good example of how we should have peace in the middle of a storm. Jesus was sleeping while the storm raged. After His scared disciples woke him up, He said they were afraid and had little faith, and then He got up and rebuked the winds and the waves, and it was completely calm. The men were amazed and asked, "What kind of man is this? Even the winds and the waves obey him!" (Matthew 8:23-27). Christians must learn that their peace is not negotiable as it is part of our benefits in the Kingdom of God.

Joy

The joy of the Lord is our strength. Paul admonished Christians to rejoice in the Lord (Philippians 4:4). There are many reasons to be joyful in the Lord but the biggest reason is the Lord Himself. That is why Nehemiah said to his fellow Israelites to avoid a particular grief, for the joy of the LORD is their strength (Nehemiah 8:10). In Psalm 126:1-3, the writer recalled that when the Lord restored the fortunes of Zion, they (the Israelites) were like those who dreamed. He noted that their mouths were filled with laughter, their tongues with songs of joy. They were so happy that other nations said God had done great things for them, and that was why they were filled with so much joy.

As already noted above, the nature of God is so good that everything about him is goodness. Being joyful is associated with good things like progress, winnings, receiving an appointment or promotion, getting married, having a baby, graduating from school or program, overcoming a challenge, and in general receiving one type of good success or the other. The joy of knowing that we are God's children and that it is Him who is doing all these wonders in our lives tends to rejuvenate His people. My wife said that when she received the Lord in 1974, the joy she, her twin sister and a friend received was so much that they felt like flying. Jesus' disciples had this type of joy during His ascension. After He had blessed them and ascended to Heaven, they worshiped Him and returned to Jerusalem with great joy (Luke 24:52). It is God who gives this type of joy to His children. Therefore, God's children enjoy an immeasurable amount of joy in His Kingdom.

It must be noted that this joy has so much depth and power that it can overshadow some of our emotional challenges as we navigate this world. One of them is the problem of depression which affects millions of people these days. The illness of depression can be healed or significantly minimized by the joy of the Lord if Christians understand the Originator and Author of their joy. Proverbs 17:22 says that a cheerful heart is good medicine, but a crushed spirit dries up the bones. Jesus Christ is the source of great joy to His people. Just thinking about Him and meditating in His name can transform a sad heart into a happy one.

Salvation

God's Kingdom is the only one that truly gives people a second chance to repent from their old ways. In it, mankind is given the opportunity to turn from a bad and wicked life of sin and helplessness into a life of holiness and hope through the forgiveness and graciousness of God. Millions of people have experienced this transformation. Jesus said in Luke 15:7 that there will be more rejoicing in heaven over one sinner who repents than over ninety-nine righteous persons who do not need to repent. In Matthew 28:19-20, Jesus commanded His disciples to go and make disciples of all nations, baptizing them in the name of the Father and of the Son and of the Holy Spirit, and teaching them to obey everything He has commanded. This command has been ever expanding, leading to the salvation of millions of people worldwide.

Throughout the ages, there have been tremendous missionary and evangelistic activities all over the world, resulting in millions of people of all cultures and nationalities repenting and accepting Christ as their savior. Numerous Christian ministries have sprung up over the years to help in preaching the Gospel to everyone that can be reached. And millions of churches, Christian organizations, television and radio ministries, and others are actively preaching the salvation message.

God's Will

One of the easiest ways of knowing about God's Kingdom is by knowing His will. God's will is always in agreement with His Kingdom. God's plan is to establish His Kingdom on earth. And He wants everything about His Kingdom to be good.

One of the lines in the Lord's Prayer goes like: "Thy will be done, as it is done in heaven". There is no evil plan, thought or deed in heaven where God's throne is. Heaven is all about righteousness, the nature of God. It is said that there is no weeping or sorrow there. And there is no night there because

Jesus or the glory of God will be light there. Heaven is so perfect that no evil can fit in there.

God's children who obey Him are in line with His Kingdom. They are the ones whom Jesus referred to as the salt of the earth. These Christians let their light shine before men and women. They are the main reason this world is still standing. Without them, this world would have been destroyed like Sodom and Gomorrah. Can you imagine a dark world full of every kind of sin and evil? The evils we witness and hear about in our present world will be nothing in comparison to such a world in which everyone would do just about any evil thing imaginable. Even if God doesn't destroy it, pretty soon it would be reduced to about only the last two remaining most wicked and powerful folks, one of whom will eventually destroy the other and then find a way to destroy himself because he cannot survive alone.

Sometimes, it is not easy to do the will of God. At such times, we are urged by friends and all to do the obvious. We should know that doing anything that is contrary to God's will does always end in a disaster or in a way that does not give us the expected result. Abraham learned that the hard way when he married Hagar his Egyptian maid who bore him Ishmael his first child. King David learned that the hard way when he went to bed with Bathsheba, another man's wife. He later had the woman's husband murdered trying to cover up his sin. These sins resulted in a chain of evil consequences in his family, too much to bear for a man who was said to be a man after God's own heart.

While we are eventually forgiven and reinstated after veering from God's will, the fact is that our disobedience results in much unnecessary drawback, heartache, hardship, pains and sufferings to us and the Kingdom of God. A good soldier is supposed to be prepared for battle and to be moving forward and not backward. The sin of disobedience to God's will almost always brings unnecessary consequences to Christians and to the coming Kingdom.

It is also important to note that all good works are not God's will. Sometimes people do good works for the wrong reasons and intentions. The Devil does that as well in order to deceive as many people as possible. People have been known to give gifts to others in order to entice or trap them. The Devil uses similar tricks to trap those who listen to him. It is important that Christians weigh the pros and cons of everything before giving in.

Faith

The Bible stated that without faith it is impossible to please God, for anyone who comes to God must believe that He is and that He is a Rewarder of all those who diligently seek Him (Hebrew 11:6). Christianity itself is based on faith in God's Son Jesus Christ and what He did at Calvary. Therefore, God's Kingdom should be a place of faith. His children will have faith in Him, and believe that He will fulfill everything He has promised. The Bible also stated in Romans 1:17 that the just shall live by faith. The just are the children of God, and they all live in this world.

Also without faith, it will be difficult to live successfully in this world. The faith of the children of God enables them to overcome all sorts of challenges and roadblocks in this world. Our faith in Jesus Christ enables us to scale any wall, overcome all mountains, and find a way where there was no way. The great men and women of faith listed in Hebrews 11 were famous, and are examples to us today because of their wonderful faith in God. Through faith, they overcame unimaginable odds and moved great mountains.

Abraham demonstrated great faith when he believed God for a son in his old age, and when he believed God for the nation of Israel. While the nation was never realized while he lived, his belief and faith that it would be realized became a reality when Joshua and the Jewish people fought and drove out the Canaanites and occupied their land. Our Lord Jesus Christ demonstrated an unequaled faith when He founded the Church two thousand years ago. His Church has grown and permeated every aspect of the world today. It has become the most popular, prolific, prominent, powerful and populous religion in the whole world. It has done more good to mankind than any other event has in human history. And the Bible stated that God spoke the world into being. He did it by faith because He is the Author and Finisher of our faith.

Light

The apostle John described how God's light shines and the darkness has not overcome it (John 1:5). The Word of God brings light to many hearts. It has liberated millions of people from the world of darkness. It brings truth and helps men and women to see the truth and live.

There was the story of some primitive African communities who used to kill their new born twins on the ground that it was an abomination for a woman to give birth to multiple babies in one pregnancy. In such dark communities, superstitious beliefs made humans to act like non-humans. Sometimes humans were sacrificed to gods and evil spirits. But when missionaries from America and Europe arrived, these evil practices were stopped. Hence we sing: *Arise and shine, for your light has come…* (Isaiah 60:1).

The Process of Personal Restoration

Personal restoration is the process of turning a life setback to a happy, progressive, godly life. Often, the setbacks are tragic life occurrences that took place when people (Christians and non-Christians) have erred. They can result in things like losing one's job, career, position, appointment or business; damage to one's reputation; loss of good health; damage or loss of one's family; loss of good or trusted friends; loss from economic downturn, natural disaster, or just general disappointment in life because of a feeling that one is not where he or she had expected to be in life.

Dealing with any one of the above situations takes time and commitment. In other words, it is a process that works its way through the period of our commitment to playing our role as we work with our Heavenly Father through the healing and eventual restoration of the damage. We must, with commitment and patience, work with God who will see to it that we are restored. It may take days, weeks, months or years, but it will happen if we remain faithful to our Father.

The first consolation to everyone reading this book now is to understand that just about everyone in life goes through one or more of these. Some folks experience them more than once in life. History is full of people, in particular children of God, suffering all sorts of setbacks and, most often, getting restored fully or better than they were before the experience. Notable examples included people like Joseph who was sold by his brothers as a slave; Moses who lost his royal status and became a fugitive in another land; King David whose boss King Saul hunted him to assassinate him, and later David's own son Absalom tried to kill him in his bid to wrench the kingdom of Israel out of his hands; Daniel who went from a prince to becoming a slave in the land of Babylon; little Esther who was a slave girl with her uncle Mordecai in the land of Shushan; Hannah who was barren for so many years while her husband's other wife made fun of her; and the apostle Paul who was almost rejected by both Jews and some apostles when he was first converted to Christianity. All these folks eventually turned their situations around and became great pillars in the history of God's Kingdom.

However, a common element of life restoration is that it takes time, sometimes months or years to fully be accomplished. Most of the persons mentioned above took some years of their lives to fully restore their situations to or above what they should have been. For example, it took David some years of running and hiding from King Saul to later becoming a king himself. Moses served his father-in-law

Jethro for some years before receiving the call to go and liberate the Israelites out of Egypt. And it took Hannah years of torment on her barrenness to receiving the promise of actually having children herself. Sometimes, the period of restoration can be shorter, but often the nature of the situation plays a role in the duration of the restoration.

The above warriors also all have a few things in common. For one, they all went through a life-changing process. The process of life restoration is like the potter's wheel experience described in Jeremiah 18. Damaged lives are like broken or damaged vessels (pots). The Lord who is the true Potter gathers our broken pieces together, forms the clay lump and remolds it into something more beautifully precious.

If you have ever watched a skilled potter work with a potter's wheel, you would notice that the process is a detailed, highly skilled one. First, the clay lump, which has already been prepared, is placed on the table or platform called the wheel. As the wheel spins, the potter uses his or her hands and fingers to work the spinning lump into a desired shape or form. Often, the potter performs processes like pressing, carving, flaring, and trimming using the fingers and other tools. These processes help to add the desired shapes and features.

In each of the above processes, the clay never tells or complains to the potter how it feels. The clay is completely pliable or surrendered to the potter's will. The potter is the master and the clay is his or her material. The master molds the clay into something beautiful at the end. While the cost of the clay is usually not high, many of these clay end products sell for much higher prices.

Drawing from the clay example given above, we can see several analogies that clay has with the heroes of faith mentioned above. For one, they all loved God. The love for God helps His children to trust Him during times of great oppression, downturn, loss or defeat. God's children know that there is no other place to go to in times of trouble. They know that their Master holds the whole wide world in His hands and will find a way to restore them back. The love for God has a soothing effect during times of setbacks. For many matured Christians, tragedies or setbacks hardly rock them. They tend to be immovable when hard times come. Two good examples are Paul and Silas who, after being whipped and thrown into a jail, started singing inside the jail to the amazement of everyone (Acts 16:22-28). Paul also was as bold as a lion during the famous shipwreck while he was being taken to Rome for trial. He was the only person on board who encouraged the sailors and maintained that all would be well. When bitten by a snake after the shipwreck, he simply flung the snake into the fire. The psalmist noted that those who trust in the Lord are like Mount Zion, which cannot be shaken but endures forever (Psalm 125:1).

Another common thing with these warriors is the resilience and persistence of their faith during their struggles. The Bible made it clear that without faith it is practically impossible to please God. During a time of restoration, we must remain strong and have faith in God. We must refuse to give in to the enemy who is fighting to see that we lose. We must believe that God is able to reward us in the end. What some folks don't realize is that something is happening in the background while we are waiting. The person waiting may not be able to see what is happening, but God sees it all. In due time, He will allow us to see what He has done.

This chapter has dealt with the topic of the Kingdom of God's other characteristics, including miracles, peace, joy, progress, faith, light, His will and salvation. These characteristics are embedded in the other chapters of this book, but are specifically discussed here to point out their prime position in the Kingdom of God. This chapter also discussed the process of personal restoration, to aid other pilgrims who are on the march in the Kingdom. Personal restoration should be seen as a normal part of Christian life, and is critical for our continued growth and maturity in the Kingdom. The next chapter will examine the various types of opportunities in the Kingdom of God.

CHAPTER 8

Opportunities in the Kingdom of God

As you read this chapter, you will observe that the lives of the individuals described in it have certain peculiar characteristics which set them apart. Some are gifts while others are attitudinal.

Opportunities can help open doors to activities and events that create or generate new careers, jobs, promotions, products, services and trends in a society. They can have personal, family, local, national or international dimensions. In each case, they bring significant blessings to God's children and His Kingdom. Opportunities in God's Kingdom are expressed in the forms of solutions to the needs of God's children in society, needs that Christians can help to meet, roles that should be performed, and preparations that should be made. Sometimes we are inspired to see these opportunities. Sometimes it takes prayers, circumstances, Divine intervention, or people around us to see them. Sometimes they are apparent, but sometimes they are not so apparent.

Finding and taking advantage of these opportunities demand humility, vision, and preparation. Sometimes we may have to go to some school or subject ourselves to some training. Paul and just about all the apostles went through a period of training before they became apostles. Elisha was trained by Elijah before he became the great prophet that he was. Just about all the well-known people of our time underwent some type of professional training before starting out their careers.

Opportunities can be leading us to areas of life where we have tendencies to try out as a career, explore or help out in some ways. Sometimes, it takes trying out opportunities to know whether they are what we want or not. Often these tendencies are a result of our gifted and/or learned skills, or our gifted and/or learned talents. Opportunities can be business, career, educational, family, community and other personal or corporate benefit-oriented revelations, enlightenments or empowerments.

Opportunities can also come from painful experiences or bad situations. For example, by the time they came out of Egypt, the Jews had lived in Egypt for over 400 years and reached a population that formed a great army large enough to face mighty nations. But the process of growing that mighty army was never sweet – it was mixed with torture, suffering, and much waiting. Even when their deliverer Moses finally showed up, the suffering had reached to a point where the Jews were basically slaves to the Egyptians. But the Bible said that when Balak the king of Moab and his people saw all that Israel had done to the Amorites, they were terrified because there were so many people. Indeed, Moab was filled with dread because of the Israelites (Numbers 22:2).

Opportunities and God's Kingdom

Opportunities in God's Kingdom are always associated with doing His will which, as we have seen from previous chapters, is seeking His Kingdom first. God's opportunities go in tandem with seeking His Kingdom and His righteousness. His Kingdom is broad, and so are the opportunities available to the Christian. As will be seen in the examples used in this chapter, His blessings are also attached to those opportunities. The Christians who discover and take advantage of these opportunities are always happy and blessed beyond measure.

Also it is noted here that opportunities in God's Kingdom are for the benefits of His Kingdom and His people. God's opportunities should not be harnessed, exploited and used as worldly folks do. God expects His children to use every opportunity given to them for His glory. We should know that all opportunities are His and should be used in a way that pleases Him.

Opportunities in the Lives of
Men and Women of Faith

The Christian's life is full of opportunities. One need only look at the life of Christ to see some of them. For example, when He met the Samaritan lady at Jacob's well, He saw it as a wonderful opportunity to share the Gospel with an entire village (John chapter 4). When He first met Peter his disciple, He saw an opportunity to sow in a man who would later be one of the pillars of the early Church. When He saw the cross looming from a distance, He knew it was an opportunity to permanently plant the most powerful and most populous religion in world's history. Jesus' life was full of opportunities, and He used them very wisely and effectively, knowing that His time on earth was short. And as will be seen in the following sections, His disciples saw the need to use every opportunity available to them for growing Christianity.

Hebrews chapter 11 listed people of faith who used opportunities before them to move mountains in the Kingdom of God. Biblical folks like Abraham, David, Daniel, Esther, Rahab, Joseph, Noah, and Caleb all believed God and accomplished great feats through their faith. In our modern world, many scientific inventions and discoveries have come about through research as God empowers Christian scientists and engineers to explore and venture into new frontiers of knowledge. It is no secret that our world has benefited from the increased scientific discoveries, as these discoveries are turned into new and modern products that mankind needs to enjoy life and also to live a more productive life. It is God who makes these discoveries possible through the knowledge with which He blessed mankind. It is no secret that the majority of these scientists have come from Christian and Jewish nations.

The story goes that former United States President Abraham Lincoln was once present at a place where slaves were being auctioned. As he watched the auction, he vowed to himself that if God made him the President of the United

States he would work to stop the slave business. When he finally became the President of the country, Lincoln was instrumental in working to institute a law that freed slaves in the country, a law he presented as the Emancipation Proclamation on January 1, 1863.

Characteristics and Case Examples of Christian Opportunities

The opportunities in the world are similar to the opportunities in the Kingdom in many general ways. This is because God created the world including the things in it and the opportunities generally generated by them. The basic difference is that these opportunities are not only inspired by God Himself, but also He helps His children to find them. It is God's will to reveal a secret to His children (Proverbs 25:2; Genesis 41; Daniel 2).

The opportunities the Lord has made available are for the joy and peace of His children. While they are all faith-based, they are provided out of His love for us. And they should be used with all glory given to Him. Opportunities are entangled in God's laws and tend to have any or a combination of the characterizations discussed in the following sections.

Miraculous, Divine, and Creational Opportunities

The opportunities in this cluster are often new and emerge out of God's will to create or cause something new to be generated for the benefit of man. In this group, it takes nothing other than sheer love and grace of God to cause the opportunities to arise.

Consider the cases of the miracles of separating the waters of the Red Sea, the appearance of waters at Meriba, the feeding of the Israelites with mana, and in fact all the modern day and biblical time miracles. All the Divine healing miracles of our day can also be included in this group. And in each case, God used miracles to create opportunities for His children to escape from their enemies, survive from thirst or hunger, and regain their health.

Elijah and Elisha Case Examples: Elijah and Elisha were Jewish Prophets noted for the miracles they performed. Both prophets performed many miracles and were used by God to call Israel's attention to God. Elisha was recruited by Elijah (1 Kings 19:19-21). Elisha served his master until he was taken to heaven by a chariot of fire.

The book of 1 Kings 18 narrated the contest at Mount Carmel between Elijah and the prophets of Baal. In this contest, Elijah clearly defeated and slaughtered the prophets of Baal. Two major miracles took place there: the unusual consuming of Elijah's sacrifice by a fire sent by God, and the unusual downpour sent by God after three and half years of drought. In each case, Elijah had prayed and God answered. The main purpose of these miracles was to call the Israelites back to their God.

After Elijah's departure from the scene, Elisha took his mantle and performed many miracles. One of Elisha's great miracles was the healing of a man called Naaman. Naaman was a general in the Syrian army who had the disease of leprosy. It took a lot of humbling and convincing to get him to visit the prophet Elisha for his healing (2 Kings 5). This miracle had such a profound effect on the Syrian general that he believed in God and begged Elisha to allow him to take as much of Israel's earth (or soil) as a pair of mules could carry to his land of Syria so that he could worship the living God. In this miracle, Elisha used it as an opportunity to show Naaman and his Syrian folks that there was a living God in Israel.

Modern Day Case Examples: While God has used the far reaching hands of technology and modern knowledge to solve some of man's problems like diseases and increased life longevity, the fact is that miracles and Divine interventions are still parts of our modern lives. Many Christians and even some non-Christians still testify to numerous miraculous occurrences and God's interventions in their lives today, events that helped to alter or change the directions of their lives for good. In many of these cases, opportunities for good health, deliverance from death or other problems were realized. This author has personally witnessed countless numbers of occasions of healing, deliverance from death or harm, and numerous other occurrences that could not be explained in any other way short of miracles or Divine interventions.

Attitudinal, Gifted, Inspired, and Calling Opportunities

Some opportunities are discovered by the right attitude. Some people have better attitudes than others. This is more spectacular in some folks than in others. In certain conditions, the attitude can be so pronounced that it can be described as a gift or talent of the individual. The right attitude can also enhance an inspiration to understand or know the opportunity. This knowledge is sometimes referred to as a calling on someone's life. There are talented or gifted people in the world at any time. Just about every area of human activity has folks who are more exceptional than others. When these talents are channeled to the opportunities from God, they can become tremendously useful to the Kingdom of God.

God blessed Esther with unusual beauty and attitude which attracted the eye of the King during the Jewish captivity in Shusha. As the Queen, Esther had the leverage which ordinary folks didn't have to muster the courage to approach the King to ask for a favor on behalf of the Jews. Her bravery helped in the favor to save all the Jewish people from the plot to exterminate them in the Province of Shusha (Esther 7).

Joseph was a very gifted young man. He had the gift of interpreting dreams. Besides that, he was a very godly young man. He had good attitudes and presented himself well. His godliness landed him in jail because he would not allow his master's wife to entice him to commit adultery with her. But his gift of interpreting dreams helped to launch him to become the Egyptian Prime Minister when Pharaoh elevated him after he interpreted Pharaoh's dreams. This elevation resulted in Joseph bringing all his extended family members to Egypt where they settled for over 400 years.

King David Case Example: King David was said to be a man after God's own heart. He loved and feared God so much that he was willing to do anything to please God. Whenever he sinned, he was always quick to repent. And when God punished Israel for his sin, he would offer himself to be punished instead of the people. No Israeli king did so much to bring his people closer to God than King David.

Before David became king in Israel, his predecessor Saul was king. Saul was the first King of Israel. He was full of arrogance and did not obey God as was expected of him. He disobeyed the prophet Samuel who had anointed him to be king of Israel. He jealously chased and sought David to kill him. He killed God's innocent priests. Finally, he and his three sons died in a battle with the Philistines. After his death, the people anointed David to be the king of Israel.

One of the first things David did as King of Israel was to bring the Ark of God home from the house of Abinadab where it had been kept for 20 years. The Ark was always central in the lives of Israelites. But King Saul never entertained the notion of bringing it home to where it should be. It was King David who first came up with the idea (2 Samuel 6). David brought the Ark home with much celebration and praise to God. It was said of him that he danced before the Lord with all his might on that occasion (2 Samuel 6:14).

King David later housed the Ark in a special tent he had constructed for it. He also proposed to construct a temple for the Lord where the Ark would be housed. While it was his son King Solomon who later built that temple, it was King David who came up with the plan and provided a blueprint that was followed to build Solomon's temple. King David was also instrumental in appointing the gate keepers, singers, priests and all the officers that served at the temple. He taught his people how to praise God, and he composed many psalms for this purpose. He made sure God had a prime position in the lives of the people of Israel. In Psalm 57:5, he proclaimed: "Be Thou exalted oh God above the heaven, let Thy glory be above all the earth."

As a result of David's dedication to the things of God, God promised him that his kingdom would never end! (2 Samuel 7:16). This promise held on for many years and resulted in the Savior Jesus Christ being born into David's lineage. King David himself became a very successful King of his time. It was said that he was the greatest King of the then known world. He conquered many kingdoms and expanded Israel's borders more than ever. His son and successor King Solomon became the riches and wisest person that has ever lived on planet earth.

In sum, King David (by nature and attitude) saw an opportunity in organizing the people of Israel around their God. He saw the need to enthrone God in Israel and make Him known all over the earth. He had a personal relationship with God, and would not make any decision without asking God first. He believed in God with all his heart, and God honored him and his dynasty.

Modern Day Case Examples: Our world is full of gifted and talented Christians. Some are using their gifts and talents, but some are not. The Church needs to see more of the talents given to God's people. There is a great need to place more talented and gifted Christians in secular service areas, including education, business, engineering, hospitals, corporations, governments and just about every place where talented services are needed. Any Christian who does not know his or her talent and gift should ask the Lord to reveal them to him or her. The Kingdom of God needs every hand at this time when so much work needs to be done. The opportunities are endless.

Deliverance, Change, Favor, and Release Opportunities

Often, God gives deliverances to His children. His favor can come at any time on His children. It is never His joy that His children will continue to be in captivity or bondage. That is why He takes joy in coming to the aid of His children. Often, this kind of opportunity takes the shape of deliverance, change for good, favor or release from the captivity. Psalm 126:1 said that when the Lord turned again the captivity of Zion, the delivered Jews were like those that dream. It is the sweetest experience to be delivered from our captivity or anything that is holding back our progress. Deliverances in this group can be healing, change from an unhealthy condition, or release from some form of dead end or wickedness.

The Demon-Possessed Man of Gerasenes Case Example:
The Gospel of Mark contained the story of a demon-possessed man that Jesus healed in the region of the Gerasenes. This man lived among the burial caves and could not be restrained. He was so strong that he could snap his chains and shackles. He wandered among the burial caves and in the hills, howling and cutting himself with sharp stones (Mark 5:5). This man was so possessed with so many evil spirits that his name was called Legion.

115

But when Jesus met this man, there was such a profound change in his condition and in other people and animals in the area. He was changed and his mind returned to him, much like the experience of many hallucinating drug addicts who get healed and their minds return to normal. Some 2,000 pigs plunged down the steep hillside into the lake and drowned in the water. The healed man was perfectly sane and was dressed like normal men. As Jesus was about to leave the area, this healed man begged to go with Him. But Jesus advised him to go home to his family and tell them everything the Lord has done for him. So this man started a ministry in the area proclaiming the great things Jesus had done for him; and everyone was amazed at what he told them (Mark 5:18-20). This incident was atypical about how some ministries began. What an opportunity.

A Young Man's Case Example: There was a young man who participated in the opportunities in God's Kingdom from familiar but little publicized activities. He was working for the government after finishing high school, but actually had a deep hunger to go to college and continue his studies. He had wasted some years of his life because of wars and corruption in his third-world ill-managed country. Eventually he was admitted to a college, and he had to quit his job in order to attend. He was about 24 years old at this time and had not really accomplished anything in life.

But he also had something else in mind, something that was equally deep in his heart. He wanted to start a student Christian fellowship in his new college. The school was just founded by the government and he would be one of the first students to attend it. Before he went to study at the school, he was able to acquire numerous Christian tracks which he wanted to distribute to his fellow new students as he publicized his plan on campus. He carried these tracts in his shirt's pocket as he walked around the campus. He met with and befriended many students and shared these tracts with many of them. He also met several Christians who liked his idea. Together, they were able to call the first meeting of Christian students. From this first meeting, there followed other meetings leading to the formation of his dream fellowship.

But this young man studied in his new school for only five months. It was not long when he got the news that he had won a two-year government scholarship to study in the United States. This gave him the opportunity to go to the United States of America where he continued his studies. Meanwhile, while he was starting the Christian fellowship, he had met one of the Christian girls who was also helping him to start the fellowship. This girl eventually attended the same college where this young Christian man was studying in the United States. It was at this school that they discovered it was God's will for them to marry. They also started another fellowship at their new American school and made many of their fellow Africans to be Christians and co-laborers in Christ. Their lives continued to blossom ever after.

But it took this young Christian many years to make the connection between working in God's Kingdom and what happened to him. After God delivered him from his directionless life, he saw an opportunity to do a Christian work in his college and took it, not even thinking there was a reward for serving the Master. He ended up getting a dose of blessings which included a two-year scholarship, a paid trip to the United States, a wife and much more.

Sacrificial, Painful, and Out-of-Hardship Opportunities

This group of opportunities is often seen in hardship or painful experiences. Many God's children sometimes go through a period of hardship. Often, there is much prayer on the part of these folks but the waiting continues for different lengths of time. Sometimes, the suffering goes on for many years until the answer to their prayers arrives. But usually, while they wait for the answer to arrive, the experience of carrying the burden or condition is not a pleasant one.

Hannah and Ruth Case Examples: Hannah and Ruth went through periods of utter hopelessness before they received the opportunities that literally changed their lives for good. The ordeal of Hannah with childlessness problem was recorded in 1 Samuel 1. Her husband Elkanah had two wives, Peninnah and Hannah. Peninnah would provoke Hannah about her barren condition till she wept. Hannah prayed on and made a vow that if the Lord Almighty looked on His servant's misery and remembered her and gave her a son, then she would give him to the Lord for all the days of his life, and no razor would ever be used on his head. The rest was history because it was not long after that prayer that the prophet Samuel was born, and what an opportunity he fulfilled in Israel. He was the one who anointed Saul and David to be the first two kings of Israel.

The story of Ruth actually preceded that of Hannah. She was a Moabite woman but was married to an Israelite man whose mother was Naomi. Naomi and her husband Elimelek had fled to Moab with their two sons because of a famine that had struck Israel. While there, their two sons married two Moabite women. But her husband and two sons later died in Moab, leaving Naomi and her two childless daughters-in-law. When Naomi learned that the famine in Israel was over, she decided to return to Israel. One of her daughters-in-law Ruth decided to return and live with her (Ruth 1:16-17). Upon their return to Israel, Naomi told her neighbors not to call her Naomi but to call her Mara (bitter) "because the Almighty has made my life very bitter" (verse 20).

But upon their return and settling in Israel, the two women discovered that starting out was tough. That was when Ruth told her mother-in-law to let her go to the fields and pick up the leftover grain behind any harvester in whose eyes she could find favor (Ruth 2:2). She ended up picking the leftovers in a field of a man called Boaz who happened to be a close relative of Naomi's husband. As events unfolded, Boaz ended up marrying Ruth who bore him a son named Obed. This son later became the father of Jesse who was the father of King David (Ruth 4:17). And as their genealogy showed, the Lord Jesus Christ also came from the same line.

Modern Day Case Examples: Many Christians of our modern time experience life's problems similar to what Hannah and Ruth went through. The problems of childlessness, barrenness, unemployment, underemployment, famine, losing a loved one, losing a business/career, people making fun of others, and long, endless waiting for things that are important to life are all too familiar to many. The good thing about the stories of Hannah and Ruth is the way God can turn any situation around for good. The key thing is to keep trusting in Him. Keep your hope alive in Him. Too often, He makes your ending situation much more fabulous than the beginning. Our God specializes in turning people's scars into stars.

Futuristic, Visionary, Prophetic and Directional Opportunities

Many of the Christian's opportunities can be said to be futuristic, visionary or directional. The reason is that such opportunities give the children of God a direction or expectation in life. The Word of God says that God's people perish where there is no vision (Proverbs 29:18). These opportunities help the Christian to plan for the future. Wise, philosophical people tend to see things ahead of time before others. Often, the events surrounding our lives will help a discerning person to know what will be potential future outlooks of the society, governments, economies etc. Sometimes, it takes a simple logic or reasoning to determine what may happen in the future. Sometimes it takes the proclamation of a prophet to reveal it.

Paul and Peter Case Example: The apostles Paul and Peter found the need to extend the Gospel to the Gentiles of the then world. The efforts of Paul and Peter in spearheading and propagating the Christian outreach and missionary efforts were unprecedented in Christianity's history. Paul was full of zeal for the Lord and would go to any part of the then known world to spread the Gospel. Peter was the first apostle to have a vision of the need to bring the Gentiles into the new religion. He mustered the courage to visit a man by the name of Cornelius at Caesarea and converted him and those with him (Acts 10). Together, Peter and Paul saw the need to bring in the uncircumcised Gentiles into the fold during the early time of Christianity. Paul actually asked the Colossian church to pray for his team so that God may open a door for their message, so that they may proclaim the mystery of Christ, for which he was in chains (Colossians 4:3).

While it was not easy for the apostles to initiate and undertake this task, it has resulted in the conversion of billions of people of diverse ethnic and cultural groups into Christianity over the years since Christ's death and resurrection. Today, thousands of missionaries are scattered all over the world carrying on similar mission. Moreover, millions of related opportunities in the construction of churches, hospitals, homes, schools and other countless facilities and resources associated with Christianity have been realized ever since. It will be no exaggeration to claim that there are millions of Christian workers in the forms of ministers, teachers, counselors and administrators who have found their career paths in these opportunities today. But it took the vision and calling of God, and the understanding and obedience of Paul and Peter to get it started in the first place.

Our Modern Day Case Examples: One only needs to reflect on the events of our time to see similar opportunities that faced Peter and Paul. Our present opportunities are diverse

– economic, social, climatic, political, business, religious and so forth. The Wall Street stock traders are experts in telling which stock would rise or fall in price tomorrow. Many investors can pretty much tell which section of the country would experience a boom in housing prices. And economists can give us a forecast of next year's economic situation in the country. While these forecasters sometimes fail to hit the target, the fact is that God's children can do a similar job if they watch and learn about the conditions of the country in which they live. Christians can equally learn how to discover, harness and make use of the opportunities made available to them by God.

Repentance, Renewal, Restarting and Turning-Point Opportunities

These are the so-called second chance opportunities which God gives to His children out of His long-standing love. God is a God of second chances. He is compassionate, gracious and slow to anger, abounding in love. God forgives all our sins and heals all our diseases (Psalm 103:3). He will not always accuse us nor will He harbor his anger forever; and He does not treat us as our sins deserve or repay us according to our iniquities (Psalm 103:8-10).

Actually, if the Lord has not provided us the opportunity of a second chance, there might not be a truly sinless child of God today. It is so encouraging that we have a Father who forgives us our sins, although He also expects us to forgive those who sinned against us. And in doing so, we open up this great avenue to tap into the types of opportunities discussed in this section.

The Woman Caught in Adultery and Zacchaeus Case Examples: Both the woman caught in adultery discussed in John 8:1-11 and Zacchaeus the notorious tax collector discussed in Luke 19:1-10 had every reason to be happy and at peace with themselves. They both lived a depraved lifestyle of sin and thus gained such bad reputations in the community. Both had every reason to be in hell, but yet it pleased the Lord Jesus Christ to save them from the direction of wrath that they were headed on.

While the Bible did not provide much lengthy information on the whereabouts of these two folks after their conversion, there is not much to be said about their later accomplishments in their new lives. However, common sense dictates that Christ did a magnificent work in their lives. It is known that the Lord saved the life of the woman caught in adultery from what would have been an imminent death by stoning. And having thus saved her, He told her to go and sin no more. But Zacchaeus on the other hand, received so much salvation that he offered to return all the money he had stolen from the public. To that the Lord said that salvation had come into that house that day.

What should be noted in these stories are the joy and peace that come to a saved life. In Psalm 51:12, David prayed to God to restore to him the joy of His salvation. In Psalm 31:2, he declared that blessed is the one whose transgressions are forgiven, and whose sins are covered. Another way to express this is how joyful is the man or woman whose sins are forgiven. Forgiveness of sin is like forgiving a poor person a very big debt that he can never pay back. David himself experienced such forgiveness after his adulterous sin with a woman by the name of Bathsheba. Therefore, forgiveness of sin from God is a wonderful opportunity to renew and restart our lives for good. A life lived with joy and happiness is much better than one lived with unhappiness and sadness.

Modern-Day Case Examples: Millions of Christians will agree that their lives are happier today than what they used to be. These Christians know that they used to live in darkness but the Word of God has brought light into their lives. A forgiven life is one of thrill in the Holy Ghost. Jesus said that He is the Light of the world, and that whoever follows Him will never walk in darkness, but will have the light of life (John 8:12). Christ is indeed a joy to His people.

Faithfulness, Trustworthiness, and Continuous Opportunities

While mankind is clearly not perfect in his relationship with God, there is clear provision of God's faithfulness to those who do their best to love Him all the days of their lives. Serving God really pays dividends, but there are those children of God who are more faithful than others. Hebrews 11 is replete with the names and accomplishments of such folks, and our modern world has some of them as well. Our God is a faithful God, keeping His covenant of love to a thousand generations of those who love Him and keep His commandments (Deuteronomy 7:9). He remembers His covenant forever, the promise He made, for a thousand generations (1 Chronicles 16:15). We are also reminded in Hebrews 11:6 that without faith it is impossible to please God because He that comes to Him must believe that He is and that He is a rewarder of those who diligently seek Him. God will never leave nor forsake such folks (Hebrews 13:5).

The opportunities that follow these folks tend to be lifelong and continuous. They may have problems like other folks, but their issues tend to be easier to manage at every juncture when compared to others. Psalm 91 notes that thousands will fall at their sides but nothing will happen to them because God will command His angels to guard such children. And because they love the Lord, He will rescue and protect them because they acknowledge His name. They will call on Him and He will answer them. And He will be with them in trouble, He will deliver and honor them, and satisfy them with long life and salvation. In other words, their opportunities are endless!

Joshua and Caleb Case Examples: Joshua and Caleb were Jewish contemporaries and also two of the most faithful men of their time. Joshua was said to be the son of Nun who hailed from the tribe of Ephraim. Caleb was the son of Jephunneh who hailed from the tribe of Judah. While Joshua was often regarded as Moses' assistant, both Joshua and Caleb were part of the 12 spies that Moses sent to spy the land of Canaan. Both men were also the only ones that gave positive report to Moses and the people when they returned. As a result, both were spared the punishment of death in the wilderness, which other spies had received for discouraging the people with their negative report.

Both men played active roles in the conquests that followed the occupation of the Promised Land. Joshua was Moses' replacement after the death of Moses. He became Israel's commander and was instrumental in leading them to cross the Jordan River, the defeat of Jericho and many other communities. He was a great warrior and hardly lost a fight. He encouraged Israel to serve the Lord instead of the god their ancestors served beyond the Euphrates and the gods of the Amorites. But as for him and his family, they would serve the Lord (Joshua 24:15). It is said that when they had finished dividing the land into its allotted portions, the Israelites gave Joshua son of Nun the land of Timnath Serah in the hill country of Ephraim as an inheritance among them as the Lord had commanded. It was the town he had asked for. He built up the town and settled there (Joshua 19:49-50). What an opportunity.

Caleb himself was also a great warrior. Even at the age of 85, he was still ready to fight the giants of Canaan. In fact, he came to Joshua at Gilgal and reminded him about the promise Moses had made to Joshua and him when he was 40 years old, about giving them an inheritance for their faithfulness. He reminded Joshua and said: *"the Lord has kept me alive, as He said, these forty-five years, ever since the Lord spoke this word to Moses while Israel wandered in the wilderness; and now, here I am this day, eighty-five years old. As yet I am as strong this day as on the day that Moses sent me; just as my strength was then, so now is my strength for war, both for going out and for coming in. Now therefore, give me this mountain of which the Lord spoke in that day; for you heard in that day how the Anakim were there, and that the cities were great and fortified. It may be that the Lord will be with me, and I shall be able to drive them out as the Lord said."* (Joshua 14:10-12).

Joshua eventually blessed Caleb, and gave him the territory of Hebron as an inheritance. It is said that Hebron became the inheritance of Caleb the son of Jephunneh because he wholly followed the Lord God of Israel. Hebron's name used to be Kirjath Arba after Arba who was said to be the greatest man among the Anakim. Caleb was able to drive out the giants in the land and occupied it with his family. Receiving a whole land of Hebron as a gift was quite an opportunity. Can you imagine receiving a whole choice city as a gift?

Modern Day Case Examples: There are thousands, if not millions, of very faithful Christians today who enjoy the opportunities of Joshua and Caleb. Faithfulness to God is all it takes to enjoy a continuous provision of opportunities in His Kingdom. King David adjourned his son Solomon to walk in obedience to God, and keep His decrees and commands, His laws and regulations, as written in the Law of Moses so that he may prosper in everything (1 Kings 2:3). There is no doubt that folks who are enjoying the most opportunities in terms of their peace, joy, love and contentment are Christians who are faithful to God. Some people think that being rich in this world's money and material things is the same as opportunities. There are millions of folks who have acquired millions or billions of dollars of these things and yet are scared, unhappy and confused in life. The opportunities that resulted in such riches most often are a result of corrupt, get-rich quick schemes of our modern world. But the riches that result from God-given opportunities are pure, honest and unbounding. These opportunities and their resultant riches are accompanied by peace, joy and much contentment.

Conclusions

This chapter reviewed the topic of opportunities that abound in the Kingdom of God. It noted that these opportunities are for the benefits of God's children and His Kingdom. However, all opportunities are for the glory of God and should be used that way. It then looked into the characteristics of these opportunities. Different groups of opportunities were examined. They include: miraculous, divine, and creational opportunities; attitudinal, gifted, inspired, and calling opportunities; deliverance, change, favor, and release opportunities; sacrificial, painful, and out-of-hardship opportunities; futuristic, visionary, prophetic and directional opportunities; repentance, renewal, restarting and turning-point opportunities; and faithfulness, trustworthiness, and continuous opportunities. The next chapter will look into the topic of how to position oneself to be a part of God's Kingdom.

CHAPTER 9

How to Position Myself to Be Part of God's Kingdom

The previous chapters have discussed the specifics of the Kingdom of God. God's Kingdom is intended for His children to occupy and enjoy. As has been shown, it has enormous benefits and is the best place to be. However, it is clear that some folks, for one reason or another, do not know about this Kingdom or how to be a part of it. This chapter is designed to help folks in that group to know how to be admitted into God's Kingdom.

There are several steps to take to be a part of God's Kingdom. The Bible clearly shows that all men have sinned and come short of the glory of God (Romans 3:23). In the previous verses of the same chapter, the writer (Paul) made it plain that under the law, no human being is righteous before God. The only way any human being can be free and come to God is by simple faith in His Son Jesus Christ who came into the world just for that same purpose. No human can save himself or herself from this hopeless situation. But, recognizing this hopeless situation, God sent His son to die for us (Romans 5:8). That is why Jesus is called our Redeemer, Advocate, the Lamb of God, Messiah, King of Peace, Lord of All, Emmanuel, the Anointed One, the Author and Finisher of our faith, and Savior. Jesus Christ Himself said in John 3:3 that unless a human being is born again, the person cannot see the Kingdom of God.

One lyric described Jesus Christ this way:

Christ alone, Cornerstone
Weak made strong
In the Savior's love
Through the storm
He is Lord
Lord of all

Therefore, to qualify as God's true child in His Kingdom, the following steps must be taken first if they have not already been taken. Only five steps are discussed here but they are broad enough to cover other areas that help one to live a victorious and happy Christian life in the Kingdom of God.

a. You must be born again (John 3:3).
b. You must denounce and abandon all the worldly evil things of the past lifestyle (Luke 11:23-26).
c. You must be serious with yourself and live a life that pleases God (Matthew 6:33).
d. Be at peace with yourself.

e. Search your life continually for what should be improved and what should not be in it.

All genuine Christians have already gone through step 1. But if that is not the case with any reader of this book, it is highly recommended that they begin with step 1, as the rest of the steps cannot happen without that step. These are distinct but different steps and they are very important in qualifying for membership in the Kingdom of God described in this book. The last four steps have been added here to help all Christians develop a more responsible lifestyle which is a key to seeing good progress in one's life.

You Must be Born Again

It does not matter what age we are, our Lord Jesus said it Himself that unless a man is born again, he or she can never see or enter the Kingdom of God (John 3:3). This is the beginning or starting point for all Christians. In verses 6 and 7, He said that flesh gives birth to flesh, but the Spirit gives birth to spirit. This means that the born-again experience He was talking about had to do with our spirit. In verses 16-18, He said that *"God so loved the world that He gave His one and only Son, that whoever believes in Him shall not perish but shall have eternal life. For God did not send His Son into the world to condemn the world, but to save the world through Him. Whoever believes in Him is not condemned, but whoever does not believe stands condemned already because they have not believed in the name of God's one and only Son"*. Moreover, Romans 5:8 reminds us how God demonstrated His own love for us in that while we were still hopeless sinners, Christ died for us. Essentially, Christ took our place so that we might not receive the punishment due to us sinners. That punishment is death.

This level of sacrifice is hardly seen amongst humans throughout history. There are folks who commit suicide bombing and that sort of thing but it is hardly to the level of love for humanity demonstrated by Christ's own death for us. His death was strictly for the salvation of mankind. He was ordained or destined for it, and He came and fulfilled it without any type of hate against anyone. He loved mankind to His last breath on the cross. No human being has ever done anything like that in world's history. And to crown it all, He rose from the dead three days afterward. Again, His death and resurrection represented Divine feats that have never been replicated by any human in the history of the world.

Jesus made it clear that to be born again is to believe in Him. Believing in Him is the result of His Spirit working in us and causing this transformation referred to as being born of the Spirit. His Spirit recreates our new spirit which shows the transformation in a person's life. That is why humans cannot understand the mystery, hence the saying that the wind blows wherever it pleases, and we hear the sound but do not know where it is coming from and where it is going (John 3:8). That is why many times friends do not understand why their friends all of a sudden join a church or fellowship of Christians irrespective of whatever promises the friends or family members made to them. That is why some born-again Christians are so excited about Christ when they meet Him. They find a new meaning in His name and fall in love with Him for what He did for them. Their eyes are opened and they immediately see the contrast between their old life and their new life. That is why they can sing songs like this one with joy:

How sweet the Name of Jesus sounds
In a believer's ear!
It soothes his sorrows, heals his wounds,
And drives away his fears.

If you think that you need to be born again now, just read these simple statements and believe them with all your heart:

Lord Jesus. I believe that you are the Son of God. I believe that you came to the world and died as a sacrifice for my sins. I believe that you rose again on the third day. I ask you to forgive me of my sins and accept me as your child. I believe that you have forgiven me all my sins. Thank you for accepting me into your kingdom. Amen!

If you prayed and believed the above prayer, then you are now born again! This is the most wonderful experience a human can undergo in this world. Unless a person is born again, everything else in this world will not really make sense. There will be no real satisfaction with just about anything we do without this experience. Congratulations! You are now ready for the next steps.

You Must Denounce and Abandon all the Worldly Evil Things of the Past Lifestyle

Jesus Himself said that "No one who puts a hand to the plow and looks back is fit for service in the Kingdom of

God" (Luke 9:62). This is a serious statement and suggests the kind of commitment Christians should make in living the lifestyle. Living a successful Christian life demands good responsibility on the part of the born-again person. The term "Christian" means we are followers and children of Christ. In other words, it means we now have Christ's character, attitude, nature, and everything that He represents. 2 Corinthians 5:17 notes that if anyone is in Christ, the new creation has come and the old has gone.

Having Christ's character, attitude and nature has great benefits of unquantifiable proportion. First, it shows we are obedient children of our Master. Being obedient to God makes Him happier than anything we can do for Him. 1 Samuel 15:22 reminds us that obedience to God is better than sacrifice, and submission to Him is better than offering the fat of rams. God loves obedient children a lot. That is one of the main reasons David was said to be a man after God's own heart. David was obedient to Him but Saul was not. As a result, the kingdom of Israel was wrenched out of Saul's hands and handed over to David.

Another key benefit of having Christ's character, attitude and nature is that it helps Christians to avoid a multitude of problems in this world. Consider the case of a man who drove his car while drunk or a woman who is stealing from her employer. The drunken man could easily hit someone and end up in jail. The stealing woman could easily be caught and end up in jail. Each of these cases could cost them time in jail, money in lawsuits and restitutions, and damage to their self-images. But Christians who do not live those kinds of lifestyles enjoy more peace and happiness because there is no need to worry about these negative and expensive consequences.

The reasons why we must denounce and abandon all the worldly evil things of the past lifestyle can be endlessly argued here. But it needs to be mentioned that God is holy and He demands that we be holy as well. Without holiness no one can see God. Therefore, anyone who does not denounce these things can never be holy and can never see God.

You Must be Serious with Yourself and Live a Life that Pleases God

This step is closely tied with the previous one about abandoning old ways and sinful lifestyle. It is a reinforcement of the previous step. In this step, the Christian is supposed to be committed and be serious with God by living a life that pleases Him. Having denounced the sinful things of the old lifestyle, the Christian should work hard to live righteously before God and man. The Lord said to first seek God's Kingdom and His righteousness, which is the topic of this book. This means seeking and doing everything that is God's will. It means making Him number one priority in your life and being obedient to Him. It means loving Him and our fellow mankind. It also means spending time with Him in prayers every day.

This step also involves being in fellowship with other Christians. It is important to join a good Bible-based church, Bible study groups, prayer groups and good Christian friends. Constant fellowship with these groups helps in the spiritual growth of a new Christian. The Bible advised that we should be involved in the assembly and fellowship of Christians (Hebrew 10:25). This practice has lots of benefits for all Christians. In this, Christians get to pray together, pray for one another, encourage one another, make friends, help one another, network with others, hear God's Word, and participate in other activities too numerous to mention here. Many of us found our spouses in such fellowships. This step also helps in our spiritual growth and creates opportunities for participation in His Kingdom.

The Process of Spiritual Growth

For growing Christians, the process of spiritual growth and development can be very challenging. Growth here also means spiritual development. It can be gradual or rapid depending on the Christian's eagerness to grow, spiritual resilience, and the Christian's level of spiritual learning curve. Some Christians give up very early in their developmental challenges, but most Christians continue the pilgrim's walk. Those challenges are why some Christians eventually yield to the forces of divorce, or abandon a promisingly lucrative career when pressure appears to build up around them. That also explains why some Christians keep on postponing promising opportunities only to start blaming themselves or someone else in later years. At the back of their minds, they are concerned about the challenges awaiting them if they engaged in those opportunities. There are many God's children today who did not attain their desired level of education, business, career, or personal plans all because they continued to push them off every time the Spirit nudged them to engage in them.

Christians must know that when the Lord called us to come, He did not mean for us to withdraw our hands from His. He is the Captain of the boat and we are His passengers. He leads the way and we are the followers. He is the Lord and we are the servants. Therefore, we must obey and follow Him in all things. We are His sheep, and He told us that His sheep hear His voice. Why then should Christians wait and not follow as commanded? He who called us will bring us to a good ending. This applies to all spiritual challenges of all Christians, whether they relate to career, family, social, business, or personal life.

All growing Christians experience spiritual growth and development in different developmental ways, but often they have a few things in common, including long waiting times, pains, and a temptation to quit or abandon the whole thing altogether. Therefore, it is very important that we keep our eyes on Christ the true Vine, know we are in a training camp, and be prepared to wait for Him to finish what He has begun in us. It has to be His way, or we will not be successful as Christians. He knows and understands what type of training we need, and He has the best tools to make us the best products after the training. We just have to obey.

Christ as the True Vine: Christ is the true Vine and we are the branches. When God prunes us, we not only produce but we produce more. One of the main purposes of pruning is to produce. The pruning process parallels the process of spiritual growth.

The process of spiritual growth progresses in tandem with a person's general progress or wellbeing in life. While it can be a difficult time in some areas, it is also one of the sweetest periods in a person's history. During this process, mountains are moved and great barriers are melted out of the person's life. This process is often slow, but the evidence is there to prove that this person is a different person and that there is some power at work behind all the successes in the person's life.

Be at Peace with Yourself

Christians should be at peace with themselves and with those around them. It is a command from the Lord. In John 14:27, Jesus clearly said that he was leaving and giving His peace to us. He made it clear that His peace is different from the type the world gives. Then He commanded us to not let our hearts to be troubled and not to be afraid.

Many Christians find it difficult grasping the meaning behind these simple words of Jesus until they have lived through some tribulations. Only then does it occur to them that no amount of worry, power, money, psychology or technical know-how could change our real peace-related situations in this world. Christ is telling us that a worry-free life is the key to living a peaceful life. He even used the sparrows and lilies to illustrate this. They do not toil and worry like humans about what to eat or what to wear, and yet our Heavenly Father takes care of them (Matthew 6:25-34).

In keeping our peace, Christians must take on the whole armor of God so that we may be able to withstand in the evil day, and having done all, to stand (Ephesians 6:13).

The full armor includes the belt of truth, the breastplate of righteousness, the gospel of peace, the shield of faith, and the Word of God. In addition, we should pray in the Spirit on all occasions with all kinds of prayers and requests. In all these, we should put our hope in God, because we will yet praise Him (Psalm 42:11).

Search Your Life Continually for What Should be Improved and What Should not be in It

No person can claim with certainty that they have no personal problems with one or more of the multitudes of areas of life's challenges often referred to as sin. These issues must be dealt with if real positive and progressive growth and development is to take place. Many times, not dealing with them in one's life can delay or even deny a Christian his or her blessings in the Kingdom of God. Some of the areas to focus on include:

- Uncontrollable anger; can lead to hate and other issues.
- Lack of self-control which can lead to violence, abuse, and other sins.
- Disrespect for authorities and others.
- Cheating in all its forms is abhorred by God (Leviticus 19:13).
- Theft or stealing what does not belong to a person.
- Not hard-working which can lead to poverty and lack of basic necessities.
- Hatred of humans who are created in God's own image.

- Unfaithfulness which can lead to divorce and other issues.
- Uncaring attitude can result in carelessness and not attending to one's own, and not helping others.
- Selfishness makes a person self-entered which has a tendency to elevate self higher than God and others.
- Stubbornness was described to be as serious as idolatry when King Saul disobeyed Samuel the prophet. Disobedience or rebellion was compared to the sin of divination (1 Samuel 15:23).
- Overeating or over drinking can result in a number of issues including overweight, heart disease, and diabetes.
- Unfairness has been described in the Bible as using unfair balance (Proverbs 20:23).
- Ignorance has been said to be a cause of perishment for God's people (Hosea 4:6).
- Sexual sins also include adultery, fornication and other forms of sexual immoralities.
- Idolatry can mean placing anything else above, or in place of, God.
- Covetousness or wanting something that belongs to someone else.
- Discord can mean participating in, encouraging or separating two friends.
- Unforgiveness or not forgiving people who offended us as God forgave us.
- Greed can lead to lack of self-control and reckless attitudes.

- Guile is a serious sin or Christ would not have described Nathaniel as a true Israelite in whom there was no guile (John 1:47).
- Irresponsibility can cause people unnecessary heartache for things that could have been avoided.
- Lies can simply be avoided by letting our "Yes" to be "yes" and our "No" to be "No" (Matthew 5:37).

Final Words

Christians are supposed to be spending time with their Master (Jesus) everyday. This is very important for new and already converted Christians, as regular fellowship with the Lord and ourselves helps to grow and enrich our spiritual lives. While work schedules do not allow for individuals and families to maintain a steady daily schedule, it is recommended that whenever possible, to have morning and/or evening (night) fellowship, devotion or prayer together. Other available times are good as well when the morning and night ones are not possible. The key thing here is to spend time with the Lord. When done in the home, it is good to have a place of meeting such as the family room, living room or bedroom. In any case, such meeting places can be regarded as the family's altar.

It must be emphasized here that spending time with our families is very important. Whatever our calling in life, ALL Christians must do their best to be in the lives of their spouses and children, as the family is the very "first" responsibility that the Lord gives to married Christians as a unit. We must manage that office very well before managing other responsibilities. Many men and women of God tend to overlook this key responsibility, but the consequences are not good for Christians. Just take a look at many past men and women of God who focused all their attention on "God's work" but appeared to do little with their spouses and/or children: Samuel the prophet, King David, and Eli the priest to name just a few. Yes, the Lord calls us to do His work, but our families are also His work. Managing our families should be the first responsibility in our lives in the Kingdom of God.

Spending time with God involves reading the Bible, praising the Lord in songs and choruses, praying to Him, meditating, sharing testimonies, discussing and teaching God's Word, encouraging each other and other activities pertinent to such a holy period. When praying, we can talk to God as our Heavenly Father. Tell Him how you love Him. Praise Him for being so good to you. Pray for His Kingdom to come. Tell Him about your needs as well. When meditating, think about His goodness, what He has done for you in the past, what He is doing for you right now, what you can do for Him, His future promises, and what He can do for you. One friend of mine from Kenya was particularly interested in meditating on the "gloriousness" of God. He would do this especially when he needed help paying his college tuition when we were students. Often, his problems would disappear in thin air before we even remembered he had a problem.

There is no official guide to reading the Bible. However new believers are often encouraged to start reading from the books of John, Psalms, Proverbs etc. Some Christians use daily reading guides prepared by some Christian institutions that have portions to be read daily. Some Bibles (one-year Bibles) have been prepared so that readers can finish the entire Bible in one year by reading daily portions each day of the year. Some of these reading guides can be obtained from churches or online sources.

It is also highly recommended for Christians to be affiliated with a home church. Find a good Bible-based church and become a member. This has a lot of benefits for Christians, including: getting to pray together, praying for one another, encouraging one another, making friends, helping one another, networking with others, hearing God's Word, and participating in other activities too numerous to mention here. Some of the best friends I have today are folks I met in churches that I had belonged to over the years.

Moreover, Christians should be social agents because many other lives are touched in so doing. But while they are friends to all peoples, they should also make quality friends, for a person is usually as good as the company they keep. It is also good to listen to good Christian music, watch decent TV shows, keep good companies, and be law-abiding citizens.

This chapter has explained how a non-Christian can be born again. It also suggested some important things a new Christian should do in order to grow in the Lord. It explained that a person must be born again in order to have a place in the Kingdom of God.

About the Author

Dr. Samuel Obi is a professor at San Jose State University, where he has taught since 1989. He coordinates and teaches courses in the manufacturing systems program in the college of engineering. God's Kingdom First, which is his fifth book, is written for everyone who really wants to see true success in their Christian life. This book explains that the secrets to living a truly successful godly life is by knowing what God's children are expected to do and doing it.

He is also the author of other books, including (1) A Table Prepared Before Me, which was written for Christians and all who want to reach their God-ordained destiny, with its aim to encourage Christians to live for the Lord the way He intends and to understand who they are and the magnitude of the table prepared before them in this journey; (2) A Handbook of Productive Industrial Ethics, an outgrowth of his background, professional convictions, and many years of interest in the field of ethics; (3) Introduction to Manufacturing Systems, a textbook for college students and everyone interested in the field of manufacturing; and (4)

Readings for Amerigerian Igbo, which was an outgrowth of his community involvement efforts for his fellow immigrants.

He has also authored numerous peer-reviewed technical articles in industrial ethics, manufacturing systems and related areas, and has presented at numerous professional conferences and events. He has served on numerous departmental, college, university, local, and national committees. He is an active technology transfer agent and consultant. Professor Obi is currently a regional director for the Honorary Epsilon Pi Tau. He has helped to found programs geared to helping Nigerian and African immigrants adjust to life in American society. One of those programs was the Nigerian Language and Cultural Institute, which he actively participated in as well as serving as the director for many years. He also helped to found and lead the Nnewi Neighborhood Association of Northern California, which has served the social, economic, and cultural needs of his fellow immigrants since 1993.

Printed in the United States
By Bookmasters